THE
HANDBOOK
FOR
BAD DAYS

THE HANDBOOK FOR BAD DAYS

SHORTCUTS TO GET PRESENT WHEN THINGS AREN'T PERFECT

Eveline Helmink

Translated by Victor Verbeek & Marleen Reimer

TILLER PRESS

New York   London   Toronto   Sydney   New Delhi

TILLER PRESS

An Imprint of Simon & Schuster, Inc.
1230 Avenue of the Americas
New York, NY 10020

First Tiller Press hardcover edition February 2021

TILLER PRESS and colophon are trademarks of Simon & Schuster, Inc.

For information about special discounts for bulk purchases, please contact Simon & Schuster Special Sales at 1-866-506-1949 or business@simonandschuster.com.

The Simon & Schuster Speakers Bureau can bring authors to your live event. For more information or to book an event, contact the Simon & Schuster Speakers Bureau at 1-866-248-3049 or visit our website at www.simonspeakers.com.

Interior design by Annelinde Tempelman, Studio 100%

Manufactured in the United States of America

1   3   5   7   9   10   8   6   4   2

Library of Congress Cataloging-in-Publication Data
Names: Helmink, Eveline, author.
Title: The handbook for bad days : shortcuts to get present when things aren't perfect / Eveline Helmink ; translated by Victor Verbeek & Marleen Reimer.
Other titles: Handboek voor mindere dagen. English Description:
New York, NY : Tiller Press, [2021]
Identifiers: LCCN 2020034578 (print) | LCCN 2020034579 (ebook) |
ISBN 9781982152765 (hardcover) | ISBN 9781982152789 (ebook)
Subjects: LCSH: Happiness. | Stress (Psychology) | Emotions.
Classification: LCC BF575.H27 H4713 2021 (print) | LCC BF575.H27 (ebook) | DDC 158.1—dc23
LC record available at https://lccn.loc.gov/2020034578
LC ebook record available at https://lccn.loc.gov/2020034579

ISBN 978-1-9821-5276-5
ISBN 978-1-9821-5278-9 (ebook)

FOR YOU,

Because at night I heard you crying,
and I didn't know quite what to say.
I found some words.

◇◇◇◇◇◇◇◇

CONTENTS

Food for Thought

The Big Bad World Out There

Everyday Light Things

Look Around for a Moment

A Tad Esoteric, But They Do Help

// **Author's Note**

This is not your average self-help book. I don't propose a method or a ready-to-use, five-step plan for your hard days. Sometimes all a bad day needs is a fluffy cardigan, a hot shower, or a nice walk. Sometimes you can keep it simple. Other times you need a little more. The shortcuts in this book are designed to make it easier for you to get started.

I am not a coach, a psychologist, or a teacher, but I've had a lifelong fascination with frayed edges, imperfection, and resilience. These days, I consider myself a cheerleader for adversity, chagrin, and discomfort, and it's my experience that although bad days don't exactly make life pleasant, they do make it interesting. They are part of life—neither good nor bad on their own. And it's often on the days when things aren't going so well that you'll learn the most about yourself. As Pema Chödrön says, "We think that the point is to pass the test or to overcome the problem, but the truth is that things don't really get solved. The healing comes from letting there be room for all of this to happen: room for grief, for relief, for misery, for joy."

I hope with all my heart that *The Handbook for Bad Days* will help you to face your worst days with courage, with compassion, and with your head held high.

— *Eveline Helmink*

// Introduction

I take the key from the ignition of my car and watch as the rain hits my windshield. In five minutes, at half past three, I will be with my mother. Which gives me five more minutes inside this steel cocoon. I already know what's about to unfold. I've had this experience many times before.

First, a feeling of resistance boils up inside of me: I don't want to, I don't want this, I want my mother to be healthy and living at home with my father. This is unfair and stupid. *Then sadness washes over me:* I don't want things to change or pass, and I want my mother back, and I want it now. *Then comes the bargaining:* She is still there—and she may no longer speak the language of words, but the language of love, which is universal and timeless. *Then the fear:* What if she's sad? What if she's not having a good day? *Then the courage:* I'll be there. *Followed by acceptance:* This is how it is.

I observe all of it and exhale. Only then do I open the door and get out.

My arms spread wide. I smile a real smile. And then I go and see my mother.

◇◇◇◇◇◇◇◇◇◇◇◇◇◇◇◇◇

In a time when we are so eager to share how perfectly our lives are going, how #blessed we are, and what a great job we're doing to get the most out of our body, mind, and soul at every moment, there doesn't seem to be much room for the inexorable truth that in every human life there are days that are, well, bad.

Days when there seems to be less of everything: less energy, less flow, and less positivity. Days when everything seems to go wrong. When, for example, you are all but certain you will end up lonely and miserable, simply because it's your destiny, and after all, all signs are pointing to the inevitable—why else would you have a flat tire? Or days when, even though nothing extraordinary is happening, you wake up with a knot in your stomach, and a faint mist of sadness is hanging around you, and whatever you do, you cannot seem to shed it. Your skin is breaking out, your hair is lifeless, and you meditate for an hour because it's supposed to help, but then you drop your bowl of yogurt and granola on the kitchen floor and conclude: *I might as well have stayed in bed.* No matter how thoroughly you search, you can't find your mojo anywhere.

Sometimes, bad days happen in reaction to things that are unfair, unexpected, or embarrassing: Your boss gives you some unwelcome feedback, or you're going through a rough patch with your partner. Other times, they appear out of the blue. It hurts, having a day when you wish you could give the finger to the merciless universe that seems to conspire against you and it feels as if the universe, in total indifference to the fate of one of its billions of earth-dwelling inhabitants, is returning the gesture. It's paradoxical, but on tough days, everything feels both incredibly personal and totally *impersonal* at the same time.

Now, I don't know about you, but the moments when I'm grumpy, irritated, sad, and/or tired are not the moments when I want to hear that I should meditate more. I don't necessarily feel like braving a rainstorm to bike to the gym or spending an hour in the kitchen to make a plant-based meal, or motivating myself to scrutinize a thick and complicated self-improvement book, however healing those things may be. On my bad days, I lack the energy. I want nothing.

When you're having a hard day, hearing about all the things you should be doing is usually not what you are hoping for. Just like you'd prefer that no one tell you that you "will find another in no time" after your boyfriend just walked out the door or that "there will be better opportunities" after you've missed out on another job. It's not that these pieces of advice aren't *meaningful*; they often make all the sense in the world. But while you may *know* there's wisdom there, that's not what it *feels* like. On hard days, it takes just a little bit longer to get from zero to Zen than on days when everything is rolling along smoothly.

To put it plainly: On my worst days I'm pretty pleased with myself if, by the end of the day, I've managed to wash my hair and not polish off the entire pint of ice cream in one sitting.

As you can probably tell by now, I have a *lot* of experience with bad days. But, of course, the great irony is that I am an editor in chief for one of the biggest happiness brands in one of the happiest countries on earth: the Netherlands. My magazine, *Happinez*, is committed to happiness, personal growth, and meaningful and purposeful living. We produce magazines all over the world, provide online courses, and organize and host dozens of events each year, including a three-day happiness festival.

In recent years, *Happinez* has inspired hundreds of thousands, if not millions of people worldwide by sharing our views on happiness and what

XVI

it means to live a mindful life. As a matter of fact, not a day goes by that I don't concern myself with these topics. I can safely say I am all about happiness . . . Not only did I turn it into my job; even after office hours, I always have happiness on my mind. Just like everyone else, I too like to live a pleasant, light, and effortless life.

So why, you might be asking, *is this woman whose personal and professional life is all about happiness writing a book about bad days? Why would someone like that be cheerleading for sitting with our disappointment, headwinds, and overall misery?* Because if there's one thing I know after a lifetime of thinking about happiness, it's that happiness is not like completing a marathon, where you cross the finish line, are awarded a medal, and remain eternally gratified. That's just not how happiness works. Happiness isn't a constant state of being. It isn't static, solid, and permanent. On the contrary, happiness is dynamic, flowing, and free.

True happiness isn't about cutting out the bad days; it's about accepting life as it is. And, in fact, it's often on those days when everything falls apart that we learn the most about what brings us comfort, resilience, courage, strength, and, yes, happiness.

However much we'd like to hold on to it forever, happiness comes and happiness goes. I sometimes compare happiness to a wild animal: You can't catch it, can't hold it in a cage, and you can't tame it. Happiness has to be free in order to be authentic.

In a world in which, theoretically, we can have anything we want, it can chafe that happiness is not something we can *possess*. Slowly but surely, the idea has permeated our society that happiness can be engineered and that, as long as you work hard enough, all your dreams will come true. Every TV commercial, talent show, and social media post is aimed at making us believe that. You are the creator of your happiness, and if you aren't happy, it is your own fault. So we pursue happiness. We search for it everywhere. We build halls of mirrors of perfection, joy, and control, only to be shocked by any blemishes, cracks, and dents. We tell ourselves that life should never be ugly or uncomfortable. Any pain or failure is to be polished away, repaired, reversed, or at least swept under the rug as quickly as possible.

You would almost feel guilty for having bad days. *Oh, you feel miserable? Such a shame you haven't managed to meditate that out of your system yet!*

I find that attitude so unnecessary. A life spent thinking in binary qualifications—happy and unhappy, perfect and imperfect, beautiful and ugly—can never be a complete one. Disappointments, discomfort, resistance, pain, and misery are part of life too. They're intrinsic to being human. Only after you've learned to accept the dark alongside the light can you really say that you're living your life to the fullest. Bad days are included. I call a life in which you are prepared to also accept lesser days and in which you dare to feel both good and bad an *inclusive* life.

You can only experience deep inner peace if you give up your forced attempts to become the "best" version of yourself, and instead aspire to be the purest, most authentic version of yourself—flaws included.

In his bestseller *The Subtle Art of not Giving a F*ck*, Mark Manson very clearly explains why the pursuit of happiness can be so contradictory. He says (and pay attention, because it really is a bit of a mind fuck): "The longing for a positive experience is in essence a negative experience. While the acceptance of a negative experience is in fact a positive experience."

Manson is speaking a profound truth there. Precisely when you learn to be present on lesser days, you will begin to experience them as positive. The forced longing for positive experiences actually is a cage: We hold ourselves captive to perfection and permanent happiness, and in doing so, we exclude so many things. The world is bigger than that. *You* are bigger than that.

If you pay close attention, you're likely to discover that this is the quintessential lesson of nearly any spiritual practice. We must accept and adapt to life as it is.

Bernie Glassman, Zen master and founder of the Zen Peacemakers, once said to me in an interview: "By freedom many people today mean the end of pain and injustice. But suffering can end, even if pain and injustice exist. Pain is located in our bodies, but the suffering is in our heads. We must learn to see life as it is: Things come and things go." Inner peace is exactly like that: The bad days don't disappear, but we accept their ebb and flow.

And the good news is: You *can* do something with bad days, however uncomfortable they may be. For starters: Don't be afraid of resistance, failure, and struggle—they're simply parts of life. Instead of learning to ignore or fight these feelings, you can learn how to anticipate them and

how to surrender yourself to them. Negative emotions don't exist to be "fixed," but to be understood. Use those sorrow-drenched phases as a chute to deeper self-knowledge: You slide down, beyond the persistent thoughts, habits, judgments, and longings.

I am (no longer) afraid of these days myself, however gray and looming they may be. Even days that seem lifeless and bleak bring opportunities for introspection, and for practicing self-love. Often my bad days direct me to the essence of things. They highlight what is not okay, what is off balance. If you welcome them in, emotions like sadness, pain, and shame are companions that can teach you a thing or two. If you are brave enough to feel and observe your emotions in the moment, you will also be able to let go of them again instead of carrying them around.

Those bad days you're so afraid of and would rather dodge are precisely the days when you can learn the most about yourself. Acknowledging your feelings, in both senses of the word, opens up space. So take a deep breath. Zoom out. What are those feelings telling you? Whenever I'm angry, it is because something is out of balance with the things I find important. My anger indicates where my boundaries lie. Whenever I'm jealous, the feeling points to something that I consciously, or subconsciously, long for. When I'm disappointed, that means that I still care about something I didn't succeed at doing or that I deprived myself of. Bad days aren't the end of the world—they're the beginning of an inward journey, gateways to a stronger, more balanced, braver version of yourself.

Examining your lesser days is not about changing or improving yourself. Rather, it's about a deep acceptance of all the things you are. About discovering your authenticity. About increasingly becoming your own true self, with all your facets, all your colors, in full presence.

There will never come a time when you no longer have bad days. But there *can* be a time when you'll be able to learn from them, and accept both yourself and the situation at hand exactly as they are. I know because I found out through trial and error.

Life can be ruthlessly dreadful. There, I said it. I may have turned happiness into my job, but life has a way of hitting you over the head and breaking your heart. It can be a struggle, I know. People can see me as the enthusiastic editor in chief, the loving friend, a creative thinker, a keen wit.

But I'm equally a divorced single mom with a dubious love life who also has a mother with early-onset dementia who can no longer live at home.

I have a more than full-time job and two young boys running around the house. I argue a lot, often talk faster than I can think (with all the attendant consequences). I make ill-advised jokes, rarely feel embarrassment, have a love-hate relationship with the gym, eat Oreos for dinner, and lose sleep over the smallest issues. Two years after I moved in, my house still doesn't have a single hanging lamp, and to be honest, I'm perpetually restless.

My heart has been blown to a thousand pieces, more than once. I have days when I cry, whine, am apathetic, nauseous, cranky, and so on. But, by now, I know that those days aren't the end of the world.

I've begun to go with the flow, like a surfer conquering a massive wave. The secret? Equal parts surrender and control. As long as you make it a habit to find some meaning or purpose in the everyday and in seemingly bad events and moods, you will resurface. When you're willing to start living your most inclusive, full life, you must blow up the dams that separate "happy" and "unhappy" in your head and heart, and allow the primal energy of each to start flowing freely. The energy of *being* as it is, in this moment.

Sometimes we call this living from your heart. Our heart doesn't tell us what is nice; it tells us what is *true*. It speaks what only you can irrefutably understand, seemingly from the core of your soul. Living from your heart isn't a quick fix for a long and happy life; it's a recipe for an honest and pure life.

I don't know how you got hold of this book, but you have it in your hands now. Welcome. It's up to you, and only you, to explore those bad days like a brave warrior, with poise and conviction. To stop running away, hiding, or buffering and to say instead *Here I am; bring it on!*

This book is not a handbook for how to avoid bad days, nor is it meant as an elaborate spiritual doorstop. My own shelves are lined with self-help books and spiritual classics that each have their own place in my life, but sometimes that deep wisdom wasn't what I needed in the moment. There are days when it's too much to contemplate the nature of suffering or the ultimate meaning of life; you just need to make it through to tomorrow.

These shortcuts aren't magical tools to circumvent negative feelings. Frankly, those tools don't exist. Be wary of anyone who wants to tell you otherwise. What you will find in the following pages are things that you can do right now, on your own, in order to tend to yourself just a little bit more on those days when things aren't going according to plan.

Ultimately, these shortcuts will help you as you learn to trust your inner compass—the one that guides you through the dense forest of emotions, habits, thoughts, expectations, and stories we tell ourselves, toward the clearings that allow the sunlight in. Life will keep handing us lemons; it's our job to discover our own recipe for lemonade.

A Note:
When It Is No Longer
Just a Bad Day

◇◇◇◇◇◇◇◇◇◇◇◇◇◇

There are bad days, there are longer periods of bad days, and then there is depression or burnout. If you remain low for a long period of time and find that you cannot put things into perspective, feel pleasure, or discover bright spots, if nothing in this book makes you laugh or smile, or if you feel like you're walking through quicksand, then it might be time to visit a professional and examine whether there's more going on. Your body can give you clues as well: weight change, loss of energy, inability to focus, sleeping badly, or dark thoughts that don't seem like you; take these signals seriously, and get help from a professional.

There is an interview with Jim Carrey on YouTube in which he clearly explains how your body starts to protest when you're depressed. When your body tells you, in Carrey's words, "I don't want to be you anymore, I don't want to be the vehicle for that avatar you created in this world, it's too much for me," pay attention. Carrey: "You should think of the word 'depressed' as 'deep rest.' Your body needs to be depressed. It needs deep rest from the character that you have been trying to play."

It's okay
TO NOT BE
OKAY

◇◇◇◇◇◇◇◇◇◇◇◇◇

FOUNDATIONS

// On Uncomfortable Feelings

There are infinite words and hashtags to celebrate happy moments and experiences. We are eager to share all that is fun, cheerful, funny, and light, just as we expect others to present us with their polished, glossy stories. When someone asks you how you are doing, "good" is the most socially acceptable answer.

The PR machine for bad days is considerably less well oiled. If we go as far as to discuss our bad days at all, we tend to give them short shrift with generalizations such as "meh," an "off day," "could be better," or the all-too-familiar "fine." We rarely elaborate or provide any nuance, preferring not to talk about the ugly, messy inner world below the surface. And understandably so! If you were to answer "How you are doing?" with "Well, not so great, actually," the room would fall silent. Your conversation partner would feel uncomfortable, the easygoing vibe suddenly gone. No one wants to spoil the party, and so we mutter "good, great!" and carry on.

But the fact that we so rarely talk about bad days also means that we quite literally lack the vocabulary to describe what's wrong. We struggle to name our negative emotions, and so we struggle to comprehend them.

Just as your doctor prefers you to point out exactly where it hurts and your hairdresser can do a better job if you can make clear what exactly you mean by "just a little off the top," a larger vocabulary for describing bad days can help you to get to the point faster.

What makes a bad day "bad," exactly? What's that gnawing sense? Knowing what you're feeling in the first place can make a world of difference, and at least it's a start to more lightness. As the wise poet Rumi wrote so astutely: "The art of knowing is knowing what to ignore." I interpret those words as: Crossing things out is getting to the essence. If you know something is bothering you, you also know what you want to examine and let go of. Therefore, before I go into further detail about shortcuts to a lighter life, we're going to review some of the language related to bad days.

Often when I think about bad days, an image of dark woods appears in my head. On those days, it can feel like I'm lost in the middle of a dense and shady forest. I enter almost unthinkingly, drawn in by an unpleasant feeling or a negative thought.

Someone says something stupid, or you sense a growing wistfulness. On and on the path winds and, slowly but surely, you begin to wander further into the thicket of your thoughts—the overgrowth is getting denser, the path narrower, with more branches and less light, until you reach the point when you've walked for so long that you can't find your way back anymore.

Getting lost in the Forest of Uncomfortable Feelings is easy. Finding your way out is the complicated part. Long ago, my brother Matthijs and I came up with a name for this feeling of being lost, when a sudden cold fog limits your sight and you can no longer see the forest for the trees. We like to call this a "weeping willow" moment. When I call my brother and tell him "Ugh, Thijs . . . I'm such a weeping willow today . . . ," he has heard enough. I have inadvertently strayed into the forest.

Often when you are worrying and pondering, your thoughts end up somewhere completely different from where they started. Perhaps even in a completely different forest, without knowing what is cause and what is effect or how you ended up there in the first place. Sometimes, for example, I feel like crying, and those tears resemble sadness, but what I'm actually feeling is intense fury. Sometimes I'm deeply irritated, but what I'm experiencing is grief over something I lost. As the saying goes, we too often lose the forest for the trees; the idea that we can see the symptoms but lose track of the cause often applies to emotions we would rather not feel.

Finding words for what is bothering you doesn't automatically mean that it will hurt less or feel less uncomfortable. Still, aimlessly wandering around in the Forest of Uncomfortable Feelings amounts to denying or neglecting your pain, which usually only leads to more pain. Naming our feelings is the first step to acceptance. It provides clarity and thus offers a ground for finding a way out—you can't find your way out of the forest if you still think you're on the main road.

Study your Forest of Uncomfortable Feelings closely. Learn how to find your way.

Naturally, in the world of psychology, a lot of research has been done on human emotions and feelings. There are countless conclusions and things worth knowing, often accompanied by diagrams, matrixes, and models. I won't exhaust you with this information; I'm not a psychologist. Generally, though, it boils down to this: Besides a set of basic emotions, we have a rich palette of related emotions, and in our complex brains, a process takes place that scientists, to this day, still haven't been able to fully grasp. Think of it like a color wheel: We have the primary colors and a whole rainbow of colors that we're fairly good at identifying. But beyond that, there is a near-infinite number of shades and hues to discover.

In an effort to better map my own Forest of Uncomfortable Feelings, I started compiling a list. For the past decade, whenever I've experienced or noticed an uncomfortable feeling, I've scribbled down the description in a little notebook. Small-scope field study, you could say. I did the same for friends and family. Whenever someone was having a hard time and tried to find words to describe a feeling, I grabbed a pen and jotted down what I heard. These words are not about what the person *knew*. On those bad days, I was primarily interested in how it *felt*, however foggy and irrational.

And guess what? It turns out there are tons of words to describe uncomfortable feelings! Look at this glossary as a tool, a reference booklet. Perhaps, on a bad day, you can scan the list to check whether one of these terms resonates with the emotion you're feeling. It's not a test; there's no right or wrong. Don't overthink it; just use it intuitively and for your own personal understanding. Uncomfortable feelings tend to blend into each other like the ink of a wet newspaper, but try to get specific. Call out negative emotions by their name. In doing so, you give them the place in your life that they deserve: out in the open, for all to hear, acknowledged. Remember this: These are only words. You feel your emotions; they don't define who you *are*.

Calling Things by
Their Name

◇◇◇◇◇◇◇◇◇◇◇◇◇◇◇◇

The Five Great Emotions
- *Anger:* when life feels unjust
- *Sadness:* when life disappoints
- *Guilt:* when you feel you're responsible for life going wrong
- *Fear:* when, perhaps, there are bears on your road
- *Shame:* when you don't seem to cut it

I feel . . . or I'm feeling . . .

ashamed // mournful // melancholy // angry // vengeful // impoverished // bitter // wistful // chaotic // lost // manipulated // ungovernable // grumpy // small // obsessed // moody // embarrassed // ridiculous // cynical // regretful // jealous // bored // numb // humiliated // unreasonable // remorseful // suspicious // confused // stunned // invisible // insecure // disgusted // sorrowful // frightened // nostalgic // homesick // sidelined // disappointed // unseen // sad // outraged // empty // punched // broken // hurt // lonely // nervous // frenetic // unbalanced // hysterical // jammed // irresponsible // overburdened // humiliated // knocked out // misunderstood // like a failure // unfairly treated // unsure // ugly // unloved // scared // aggressive // breathless // back at square one // betrayed // unsafe // despondent // wobbly // diminished // apathetic // outraged // blown down // impatient // frozen // stressed // unprotected // naked // trapped // discouraged // troubled // tired // hollow // sour // small // conflicted // limited // uncomfortable // disappointed // tearful // hateful // childish // raw // vulnerable // insufficient // cold // totally blank // stiff // uncomfortable // anonymous // gloomy // depressed // tormented // irritated // rejected // uninspired // reserved // fooled // blunted // weak // deceived // inconsistent // triggered // uprooted // tired // tricked // lazy // guilty // abandoned // distraught // untalented // stupid // cornered // stuck in a rut // meaningless // forced // indecisive // baffled // flabbergasted // upset // very, very tired // furious // fragile // desperate // done // alienated // hopeless // exhausted

// Even the Holiest Guru Has His Flaws

Oh, how we love to sanctify our heroes! It is comforting to look up to someone. We may not understand the essence of this complicated existence, but this person, so controlled, so calm, such a pure source of wisdom . . . It's marvelous when someone offers you exactly the answers that fit your consciousness like missing puzzle pieces. It's hopeful to see someone so self-actualized and authentic and loving and happy. Some teachers have that ability and are adored like pop stars by their fans and followers. They shine on social media, enchant rooms full of people, write books that will take your breath away.

We learn from the stories of others. Humans have been sharing insights and inspiration about the meaning of life since the very beginning, when we gathered around campfires and water sources to tell each other ancient stories of love and loss, pain and comfort, and good and evil.

And how wonderful that we're no longer living in an age when our personal growth depends on the stories of our ancestors or the wisdom of a random minstrel who just happens to pass by. Countless wise fellow humans are just a click away! The world and all its wisdom is at your fingertips. And there is a good chance that somewhere out there, someone has the missing insight for your mental well-being.

Thanks to my work and my personal interest, I have met, seen, heard, or otherwise witnessed in passing many wise people. I have had the privilege to go backstage with the Dalai Lama and Eckhart Tolle, have spoken one-on-one with Byron Katie, Esther Perel, and Sharon Salzberg, and have accompanied Elizabeth Lesser, Thupten Jinpa, and Mark Nepo at our festivals. My work often offers front-row seating for some of the most interesting, wise thinkers of our time. I have always thought of these experiences as educational and formative, but they also put things into perspective. "Even the holiest guru has his flaws" is a maxim, coined by my colleague Adrienne, that is regularly heard around the offices of *Happinez*.

It means: Everybody has their shortcomings, which is true. Truly ev-er-y-bo-dy. However pristine the attire, how serene the gaze, how wise their words: These are people, imperfections and all. That includes that amazing yoga teacher with her boundless energy, and that inspiring hero with his mind-blowing self-help program, as well as that influencer with the drool-worthy Instagram feed and even that enchanting writer with his poetic one-liners.

Nobody has a free pass to a carefree life.

However charismatic and inspiring they may be when in action, behind the scenes, they too have moments of being insecure, demanding, unfair, tired, and agitated. Even for the wisest master, life isn't always carefree and polished. For some people, this can be disillusioning; they may start saying things like: "exposed," "enlightened much?" or "fraud." For me, these imperfections don't tarnish the inspiration these people offer. On the contrary. Their lives offer the hope that, whoever you are, you can reach profound wisdom. No teacher, writer, sage, scholar, or guru has received an invitation to a fruitful inner life that is out of reach for others. In fact, the opposite is true. On closer inspection, many of today's most lauded and respected teachers have been shaped by their bad days: Gabrielle Bernstein and Glennon Doyle are former drug addicts. Byron Katie and Eckhart Tolle were depressed. Elizabeth Gilbert and Cheryl Strayed found themselves confronted with painful losses. The list goes on and on.

It's not just that these people found great inner freedom in spite of their pain. They found it *because* of their pain and struggle. They didn't just wake up full of wisdom and deep insights one morning. Their lives are works in progress. As Elizabeth Gilbert posted on her Instagram account: "The women I love and admire for their strength and grace did not get that way because shit worked out. They got that way because shit went wrong and they handled it. They handled it a thousand different ways on a thousand different days, but they handled it. Those women are my superheroes."

Don't let yourself be blinded or stunned by spiritual glitter and glamour. Nobody is perfect; nobody's days are all joy. It's all right to *not* be happy once in a while. When you're having a bad day, *you* are not bad. Don't focus your attention only outward; focus also on your own strength, deep inside. At the end of the day, we all go to sleep under the same dark but sublime sky.

// What Uncomfortable Feelings Are Trying to Tell You

Negative emotions have a nice quality for which they rarely get credit: They are valuable advisers. Fear, anger, and sadness feed us. "Shit is the manure of the future," *Happinez* founder Inez van Oord is famous for saying. You know, humanity couldn't have survived if it weren't for bad days. Apparently, a certain amount of discontent and drive to fix imperfection or imbalance is embedded in our DNA. This is how we survive as a species, because it is precisely by experiencing those emotions that people are forced to invent smarter things over and over again—to improve, to desire, to change, and to fight.

Our human brain is hardwired in such a way that change stimulates our survival instinct. When it gets too uncomfortable, it's time to change tack. When it hurts, that's an outright warning of danger. Experiencing both physical and mental resistance is a means to find a way forward through this mortal coil. Just think how you would grope your way through a dark space: You would avoid sharp things, whereas softer shapes would give you confidence. That's how you progress.

Now that our basic safety is much better taken care of than in earlier eras, we sometimes think that we no longer need those less pleasurable experiences and emotions. But nothing could be further from the truth; they are still a big part of our inner compass, the finely tuned instrument we use every day in order to better understand ourselves and our place in the world. Stowing away bad days or negative feelings disrupts your inner compass. It takes you out of the balance of a mysterious cosmic equilibrium in which everything has its place in a larger narrative. You could compare ignoring these alarms with pushing a ball underwater; that takes a lot of energy, and the moment you release the ball, it uncontrollably shoots up with way too much force, maybe even hitting you in the face.

I Don't Want Comfort

◇◇◇◇◇◇◇◇◇◇◇◇◇◇

"But I don't want comfort. I want God,
I want poetry, I want real danger, I want freedom,
I want goodness, I want sin."

"In fact," said Mustapha Mond,
"you're claiming the right to be unhappy."

"All right then," said the Savage defiantly,
"I'm claiming the right to be unhappy."

— *Aldous Huxley*

◇◇◇◇◇◇◇◇◇◇◇◇◇◇

Who didn't read *Brave New World* in high school? The science-fiction novel by Aldous Huxley, published in 1932, describes a perfect society, optimized through technology and science, a place where everyone is completely happy. Art, love, religion, and committed romantic relationships have all been banned; they will only lead to problems. All of the citizens use soma, a drug that makes you feel happy and relaxed. After all, frustrations and negativity will only lead to instability, and according to the leaders of the new world, nothing good can come of that.

Their ideology begins to show cracks when the protagonists begin to sense that something is wrong and decide to investigate. In the end, this is the question *Brave New World* raises: Is it better to be happy—or to be free? Is a life devoid of feelings or emotions actually worth living? Imagine that you could have a guaranteed pain-free existence at the expense of freedom and authenticity . . . What would you choose?

// Why It Is So Important to Fully Know Yourself

Look, there's nobody who, when having a lesser day, will think: Oh, what a wonderful experience this is! Can I do it again tomorrow? It's tough and exhausting to stay focused and to show up for yourself when it seems like everything sucks and there's a tumult of emotions raging inside of you. But if you make an effort to examine the dark corners and fringes of your soul, you are taking yourself seriously. It is a form of self-love to weather bad days, however contradictory that may sound, to investigate how to be calm and strong, and to be present in what is there.

When someone asks me what the key to happiness is, I almost always give them the same answer: self-knowledge. I'm convinced that understanding yourself—knowing what switches you "on" and what doesn't serve you at all, feeling what is right for you while being aware of your weak spots—is essential to navigating the daunting array of available self-help books, courses, methods, and workshops, to figure out what works for you and what doesn't. If you are looking for the key to happiness, you'll have to map your own ego.

Personal growth is never a battle with yourself. It is an embrace of yourself.

There are many roads leading inward, and not everyone travels in the same way. To quote the spiritual teacher William Bloom, who gave an interview about modern spirituality in his home in Glastonbury, England: "Try not to carry set convictions about what is spiritual and what isn't— each human being is open to the miracle of creation in their own way. Reflect on your own convictions and be open-minded about everything that comes your way. Life is a learning process, and there are many ways to explore its meaning and wonders." Amen to that.

To me, self-knowledge, self-exploration, self-awareness, and self-confidence are magical words for a lighter life. I can already hear some spiritual teachers objecting . . . "but the self doesn't really exist—now, does it?" Well. The "self" is a fascinating subject to examine, to be sure, including the question of whether such a self, or ego, serves you or even exists, but you know what? We're going to park this question for the moment.

However you wish to explore the concept of "self," for the purposes of this book it doesn't really matter. On bad days, you are stuck with yourself either way. It's one of our biggest missions in life to discover who we are and what in God's name we are doing here. And along that inward path, there's a lot to cut and prune: anxieties, assumptions, doubts, judgments.

On the path to a lighter life, at times you will have to be brutally honest with yourself. Anything that isn't true, pure, loving, or serving you is like the ivy of the soul: a persistent weed with an extensive root system and a tendency to strangle whatever it's growing on. You will have to cut it out.

Self-examination requires commitment to who you are, who you want to be, and how you want to live your life. Only you can take responsibility for how you treat yourself and the people around you. Only you will have insight into what you feel and think. Only you will know the stories you're telling yourself.

Consider self-examination as cleaning out the cluttered junk drawers inside your head, bringing order to the dusty chaos of stashed knickknacks. Ultimately, self-knowledge will become your center of gravity, your core. Inside you, there's a place where everything is balanced out, a place to which everything will always return, the calm in the eye of the storm.

Perhaps you had a wobble toy as a kid. No matter how hard you pushed it, sooner or later the figure would inevitably be standing straight. Like you. The secret is to have confidence. I call this the Law of Soul Gravity. Ultimately, you will find inner peace in the middle, where everything is balanced out. Between heaven and earth, between happiness and . . . bad days.

// You Could Call It Soul Hacking

A pantyhose sock around your vacuum cleaner nozzle to retrieve a golden earring from underneath your sofa. A paperclip to mark the edge of a roll of tape so you never have to waste time endlessly picking around for it again. Sleeping with your feet outside the covers for a better night's rest. Installing apps that force you to take breaks. Over the last couple of years, the phenomenon of life hacking has become inescapable. These tricks, shortcuts, and other clever ways to live your life as efficiently as possible minimize the time you waste on simple tasks and chores so you have more time left to do what you want.

It's a combination of time management and stress management: optimizing your life in such a systematic, practical, and smooth way that there's increasingly more room for the relaxation and gratification these methods yield.

Originally, life hacking was something for tech nerds who developed all sorts of apps to make their work faster and more effective. Today, life hacking has also become a way to cope with the avalanche of information and possibilities coming our way. Perhaps it's because its origin story involves a nest of plugs and cables, or maybe it's due to the word "effective," but life hacking is mainly a feast for the left side of the brain, where logic and reason live. The right side of the brain, the home of intuition and emotion, may have received an invitation but is somewhat of a wallflower here.

Yes, life hacks do indeed make life more straightforward, more logical, less energy draining, and maybe even easier. But often they are uninspiring and detached. Do they also make life easier to understand? Lighter? I've never found a life hack that taught me how to mend a broken heart with a safety pin.

No one has yet told me how to use that pantyhose trick to filter out bad energy. Is gaining time the same as feeling you have more space? Is logical the same as meaningful?

I prefer not to call the shortcuts in this handbook life hacks, because they are not about effectiveness, reason, or convenience. What feels more apt is the phrase "soul hacks." Soul hacks are about letting go, flexibility, and self-knowledge.

Perhaps this is the distinction between the two: Where *life* hacking is for living efficiently, *soul* hacking is living to the fullest. Soul hacking offers shortcuts to what really matters: self-love, self-knowledge, and authenticity. It's a method to more quickly and profoundly get to a place where everything is calmer and more comprehensible, an elephant path to a life of less discomfort. Soul hacks offer tools so you won't get carried away as easily by misfortunes but can be at ease with the clouds hanging over your head or the storms raging within you. These hacks put things in perspective, offer consolation, and soothe frayed nerves. They show you how much strength and resilience you're carrying within you already.

There's no better teacher than your own soul—it's a magnet, attracting what it needs and repelling what doesn't fit.

Your soul can tell you what will work for you and what won't, what will give or cost you energy, what belongs to you and what you can let go. It is your inner compass. It is flawless, delicate, and calibrated exactly to you; it guides you on your life path. Out of all the shortcuts in this book, you'll have to determine for yourself which make your life lighter and which don't. I'll tell you to get bored, I'll tell you to do something. I'll tell you that you can let go, I'll tell you to hold on. The shortcuts will give you easy-to-follow pointers on how to be mindful of the sensitivity of your soul.

You're not in touch with your soul only when lying on a yoga mat, meditating, or when hiking in a forest or making love. You're *just* as much in touch with yourself when you're angry, hurt, or tormented, when you're cursing and crying and in a bad mood. You are all parts of yourself equally; bad days give you just as much insight into your needs and who you are at your purest, most unadulterated self.

The Big Question is: *Do I matter?* It's a question that can encourage growth and self-development, but that can taunt us on lesser days: I don't belong anywhere, nobody loves me, I'm not seen, I don't have any value, and I have no control over my own life. But regardless, the answer is: You matter. It matters.

Twelve Skills That Make Lesser Days Lighter

◇◇◇◇◇◇◇◇◇◇

Intuition: alertness to the subtle whispering and deeper knowing of your soul

Self-knowledge: knowing who you are and what moves you down to the darkest corners of your soul

Attention: being present to what is, as it is

Love: experiences of unconditional connection and unity

Surrender: the art of moving along with the flow of an uncompromising life

Resilience: a ladder for climbing out of deep wells and muddy pools

Strength: firm roots that keep you grounded and nourished

Compassion: love as a verb, love put into practice

Balance: a center, a core, from which everything originates and to which everything returns

Inner Peace: a calm soul, even in a tempestuous outside world

Courage: the ingredient for living a pure and true life through trial and error

Humor: the capacity not to take yourself and life so bloody seriously

// A Foray into the Soul

I promised not to produce a spiritual doorstop, but still I'd like to spend a few moments briefly discussing the notion of "the soul." In order to keep things somewhat clear, let's agree on the following: Your soul is who you are, without masks, pretense, or appearances. Ever since the dawn of humankind, we've been trying to unravel the mystery of the soul, and there is a startling amount of information on the topic. I can tell you from personal experience that it's possible to wander the aisles of the library all night for weeks and still bike back home with a giant question mark hovering above your head.

Language can be so insufficient; the more passionately you want to define the soul, the more elusive it becomes. You can read about it and listen to people talking about it till the cows come home, but to truly learn about the soul, you must shut up and simply *be*. The words that come closest to describing how I experience "the soul" are from poet Maya Angelou, who spent her whole life embracing the imperfect, accepting hardship, and living love. When asked to define the soul on an episode of Oprah Winfrey's *Super Soul Sunday* (see, even Oprah didn't know the answer), Angelou answered, "The soul is the spirit that longs for all."

Unlike the mind, which reasons and explores, the soul is our spiritual seat—pure, direct, and intuitive. It is our essence, our connection to the larger whole, our true nature. And it is the soul that knows, that's conscious of everything that is, and that has zero interest in conditioning, masks, and role-play. On bad days, you don't want to navigate using your mind alone; you need to bring your soul along.

And when you consider the fact that the matter that makes up every single human being, including yourself, was formed billions of years ago in the universe and is being reconfigured into new forms over and over again (the notion that it's recycling itself without any matter ever being added has been well established by science), our inherent connection to the greater universe isn't so woo-woo or far-fetched at all. On an atomic level, you are part of an inconceivably vast time and space. The universe experiences and manifests itself time and time again. Things converge and things fall apart in an infinite cycle. We are part of a cosmos that is in constant flux. We *really* are made of stardust.

That longing for unity, for the balance between body, spirit, and that large whole from which we stem and into which we will vanish again—that places our quotidian struggle in a completely different perspective.

// Oh, and Don't Forget Your Body!

The third indispensable element for living a lighter life is your body. It completes the trio of mind-body-soul. On my own bad days, I take a tour of these three to check the state of affairs: What do my thoughts say? What does my soul whisper? And what does my body tell me?

If someone gave me a soapbox, I would use it to shout, "Know your body!" Because, jeez, how often it is that we take our body for granted and how skillfully we ignore what it wants to contribute. We make our body work for us, and we submit it to all sorts of things; we train, nourish, dress, and decorate our body. We force it into shapes, and fair is fair, we often look at it in a judgmental way. But do you really work together with your body? As a team of equals?

To many people's ears, the term "bodywork" sounds a little too New Agey, but there are vast layers of nuance between dancing around naked and being alert to the signals your body sends. Our body is one big radar system, one big touch screen, and one big vehicle, and grounding ourselves in our physical experience is essential to full self-knowledge.

We have all kinds of sayings that point to the relationship between our body and our mental well-being. Something being hard to stomach, for example, a weight off your chest, or a heartbreaking situation. There are all kinds of small physical alarm signals that want to point our attention to something: nerves in your gut, anger that burns under your skin, sadness that weighs your heart down. As small children, our responses are still very natural and self-evident: We cry when we fall or cover our eyes when we are afraid, and once it's over, it's over. Later, as adults, we will start to ignore those physical cues and associate all kinds of thoughts with them. The latter is especially problematic, for as long as we keep thinking, we fail to feel. In doing too much thinking, we both literally and figuratively lose touch with ourselves.

Not only can listening to your body alleviate bad days; in some cases, it can even prevent them from occurring at all. Do you know the saying "Nip it in the bud"? It stems from the idea that you should address problems before they blossom. A twinge of pain in your back? Perhaps you should take a listen. An indefinable ennui taking root? Better pay attention. It will save you a lot of hassle.

Ask someone to locate her mind and she will point to her head. It's the part of the body we associate with wisdom, and we tend to prioritize our thoughts as safe and rational. But all that thinking can hurt you too—those thousand and one thoughts, tumbling like waves, can drown you. In fact, we often experience stress and discomfort in our head: Migraines, brain fog, pulsing aches—these are common physical symptoms of very real stress. (Tip: If you're prone to these sensations and want to soothe your head, emphatically lower your shoulders and gently sway your head in a circular motion for a few minutes.)

There is, however, another part of the body where tensions are commonly felt: the stomach. When we say things like "it makes me sick," or "it doesn't sit well," we usually place our hands somewhere on the lower belly, indicating where those clear insights reside. It's a different, more intuitive knowing, but one that science has clarified and validated. In fact, it's so widely accepted that we have a term for it: the mind-gut connection.

It appears that our intestines contain neurons that, like neurons in the brain, receive, process, and react to impressions. An interesting thought, isn't it—your gut as a sort of second brain? And then to think that the gut is also deemed to be the epicenter of imaginative power, vitality, and creativity . . . As the adage goes, "follow your gut" and you may find that it's easier to navigate your Forest of Uncomfortable Feelings. This isn't to say that gut feelings are the holy grail; they might very well be based on old stories and past experiences. Even so, they still deserve your attention.

And no, your body isn't always right. Or, rather, you don't always have to agree with your body. Perhaps it's nothing more than an old insecurity reminding you that you are running a risk or an old ache that wants to be heard. Sometimes I will engage in a conversation with my body:

Thank you, insecurity; I feel you, and yes, there is a chance of failure, but I'm going to dare to take the risk. Hey there, old ache; yes, I know, we made a mistake at this point before, didn't we? I'll try do to it another way this time around—but thank you for pointing it out to me anyway.

Help Me

◇◇◇◇◇◇◇◇◇◇◇◇◇◇◇◇

While it's up to you to discover what your mind, body, and soul are saying to you on bad days, this doesn't mean that you will be forced to languish in bottomless pools of misery on your own. I learned the hard way that it's okay to ask for help. It isn't easy to accept an extended hand, let alone ask for one yourself; we are all tired and busy and wiped out. Still, dropping my "I'll be all right!" armor every now and then has done me a lot of good.

My support troops aren't standing at my side twenty-four seven. They aren't there when I splash a full pan of pasta sauce on the floor, they aren't in the passenger seat when I'm stuck in traffic for three hours, and they aren't lying beside me when I wake up on a gray Sunday morning while the rain lashes against my windows. But they're there when I call them.

Every now and then, you will need someone. That is normal. That is healthy. That is human. When you do, say the following: Help me. Help is always there, in one form or another. Search for it. Ask for it. Accept it. Remember, you may be doing another person a favor by showing your vulnerability: It may mean that they will also learn to ask for help.

Perfection *is a* MOVING TARGET

◇◇◇◇◇◇◇◇◇◇◇◇◇◇

F*CK
WHAT
MENTALLY
STRONG
PEOPLE
DO

◇◇◇◇◇◇◇◇◇◇◇◇◇◇

// But Actually, F*ck It

Life constantly puts us to the test. No matter how well you think you have things under control, you'll reach a point when things start to go against you. There are unwelcome changes at your work, your love life isn't all rosy, a friendship breaks down, your body fails—the universe tends to have its own agenda.

There are lots of sources online with tips on how to deal with unwelcome life situations. Popular among these are lists of what "mentally strong people" do. If you were to follow such tips, you would be darting and diving through the obstacle course of life like a ninja. Because that is what "mentally strong" people seem to do: They beat life wearing a suit of armor that protects them from all pain and discomfort. Bad days, however, don't test your mental strength. They demand things from the whole shebang—not only your mental discipline but also your physical energy and your spiritual strength.

Mind, body, and soul. A three-legged stool is only strong if all the legs are the same height, and focusing on just your mental ability puts you out of balance. Lists for mentally strong people lean on only one leg: control, power, command, and discipline. They totally miss out on chaos, weakness, letting go, and giving up. So whatever "they" (these so-called mentally strong people) do, f*ck it.

Seven Adages about Mentally Strong People You Can Forget about from Now On

◇◇◇◇◇◇◇◇◇◇◇◇◇

1. They keep going, no matter what, and don't waste any time on remorse, worries, or self-doubts.

That's right: onward! How inefficient to waste valuable time on feeling what needs to be felt . . . right? Well, I for one think you should be able to have a good cry from time to time. If you intend to keep forging ahead, you first need to look around to see what you're dragging behind you, and sometimes you need to let go of the need to keep pressing onward in order to take time to feel what's there. Untangle the knots. Learn from your emotions and doubts. Adjust your goals. Breathe in, and then it's time to move on.

2. They never lose sight of the big picture; they are in control and won't let go of it.

Holding the reins of your life in your hands is commendable, but mentally strong people must have very sore hands. At some point in their lives, everyone will lose some control or will have to let go. Maybe you get ill, your partner leaves you, or a loved one dies. Even the most mundane things are largely out of your control: It's pouring when you go camping, the trains aren't running when you're in a hurry, the avocados aren't ripe when you want to eat them. Life is one big exercise in letting go of control. People who never loosen the reins are generally not the best people to be around. When you can't share your power or strength or play with it, you become rigid.

The secret isn't keeping control, but learning how to gain it. When you clench a fist full of fine sand, some of it will run through your fingers. But if you hold your hand open, the sand will rest in your palm.

3. They embrace change and welcome new challenges.

People don't like change. We aren't wired that way—it's an ancient, ingrained habit of our species. Change is uncertain; uncertainty equals danger. You might be thinking, *Well I handle change well! I travel across the world. I can sleep anywhere, work for a new employer every week!* That may be so! You can get used to change; you can learn to cope with it, and you can even yearn for it. Change isn't nice or exciting per se, however. Change can also lead to insecurity, pain, and discomfort. In many cases, embracing change is a bit of a stretch. So is embracing challenges. Replace "embrace" and "welcome" with words such as "accept" and "flow with"; those are already a lot to handle, especially on a bad day. You don't have to treat every unwanted plot twist that comes along to tea and biscuits.

4. They stay positive: they never complain.

Great! How nice to proclaim, *I'm happy and that's that. This is my decision, and you'll just have to deal with it.* But then life . . . what a buzzkill, eh? I've tried to do it: biking through the pouring rain with a stubborn smile, nodding along politely upon hearing bad news, and laughing as I barely make deadlines—but it started to hurt my cheeks.

No one is happy all the time. No one can spend their life never complaining, and everyone ends up wasting energy on things we don't have any control over. That's pretty much just what life is! At best, you can have control for a time, or the illusion of control, until life presents you with the facts once again. Complaining (see p. 95 to discover the art of Advanced Complaining) is not a sign of weakness. It serves a purpose: Complaining can relax us, and it helps to contextualize and clarify situations. It demonstrates what's getting at you. It's wonderful! Complaining allows us to articulate better and more honestly what's going on in our lives than all our socially acceptable words combined.

5. They are friendly, honest, and unafraid to speak up. They are not out to please others.

If I could put together my ideal personality from a list of characteristics, "friendly, honest, and unafraid to speak up" would certainly be on my short list. It's the second part of the description that I find difficult: that mentally strong people don't concern themselves with pleasing other people. It's absolutely true that you are not required to bear the expectations and needs of others while you're walking the tightrope of your own life, but another option is balancing out the needs of others with your own. I myself cannot picture a spiritual journey on which others are by definition excluded from the considerations we make.

Lak'ech ala k'in is an ancient Mayan proverb: I am you, and you are me. It's an expression of an awareness that we are part of something bigger and that we are all one. All our actions influence everything around us. Being aware of how you can please others while still making choices for your own benefit is, placed in a bigger context, a powerful and compassionate way of life rather than a weakness. The trick is to distinguish between pleasing that can help you grow and pleasing that diminishes you, to understand when you are balanced and when you might lose your balance.

6. They weigh the risks and advantages *before* they act.

I can honestly say I have made some of the best decisions in my life *without* risk assessment and carefully weighed benefit analyses. Those decisions came from a profound understanding and a courage that cannot be explained in words. I'm not saying weighing risks is a bad idea. On the contrary, it's an excellent method for survival. The thing is that analyzing, rationalizing, assessing . . . these are all based in the mind, and we have more tools for life in our toolbox, including our body and our intuition. Making lists of pros and cons doesn't necessarily lead to the best decisions. For example, would you want to buy a house that seems like a great investment on paper but doesn't feel like home? Would you want to marry someone dull just because it's safe?

I owe my job at *Happinez* to a woman who cared about more than the numbers alone. Had it been up to the first few publishers the idea was pitched to, the magazine never would've existed, but as Inez wrote in her book *Als jouw leven een cirkel is, waar sta je dan?* (roughly translated, *If Your Life Is a Circle, Where Do You Stand?*): "Why should I have given myself over to doubt while my entire being was telling me I had to [act]?! This idea came to me straight from the center of the circle, from my heart and soul, possibly even from heaven and earth."

Intuition is what gives you the courage to persevere. Include your whole self in what you do and choose. Adjust to what you know *as well as* what you feel, but don't let yourself become stuck; keep moving. Sometimes you just have to do something first, and then find out whether it was a good choice as the process unfolds. *No hopes, no fears*, a monk whispered to me in a Thai monastery once.

7. They celebrate the success of others and aren't jealous.

Have you ever seen someone shine, wished it was you, and then felt a bit uncomfortable about it afterward? Jealousy isn't generally an attractive emotion, especially when it's tainted by anger and resentment. Still, jealousy can be a pretty accurate indication of where you are in life and where you want to go. It helps you to get a clearer sense of your goals. On the path from feeling jealous to celebrating someone else's success, there are precious few stepping-stones. Knowing what desirable behavior is and observing what is happening instead can be painful. But maybe you'll find a moment to voice your ambivalence: I'm happy for you, and at the same time, I feel that what you have achieved is what I want as well. You'll be vulnerable, but sincerely so.

Lastly, jealousy can prod you to ask an equally important question: Are you paying enough attention to your own achievements? Do you celebrate how far you yourself have come? The more you manage to be unabashedly proud of yourself from time to time, the more you'll be genuinely happy about other people's windfalls and successes. Celebrate your own achievements regularly!

// Manage the Mulling

There's no sense in ruminating all day

"Don't worry!" A classic example of an elephant-in-the-room situation. The moment you tell yourself not to think about the elephant, you can't stop doing so. It's the same with worrying: It's there, and it's not going away until you give it attention. In a sense, worrying is like crying or getting angry: If you suppress it, you know that it will find a way out eventually, often in less charming forms and at unexpected moments.

Although I hate worrying, I do it regularly. It has a sneaky way of sapping energy. You can have the exact same thought ten thousand times, in a loop. Even as you're doing other stuff, your worries remain constantly in the background, like hold music that sets your teeth on edge. On bad days, this constant noise can exhaust you before you realize it. If you don't address your worries, they won't go anywhere, as this endless loop rarely leads to a solution. Most worries aren't that interesting, because they aren't realistic, aren't important, or concern things you can't control.

The best thing you can do for yourself is give your worries your full attention. Just as you would kneel down to console a crying toddler, lend your worries a kind, warm ear. You might not always have time for this in the moment, but whenever you find yourself continually mulling over things, or if there's constant noise in your head, set aside some time for worrying. Carve out space in your schedule, and make an appointment with yourself. It sounds childish, but it's exceptionally effective.

This appointment doesn't necessarily mean assuming the lotus position on a yoga mat. Worry time needn't be a solemn ritual. Just sitting on a bench, doing the dishes, or taking a minute during a boring car ride will do just fine, as long as you let your mind wander undisturbed and uninterrupted. Fifteen minutes, half an hour, maybe longer. Set a timer, then make some tea, put your feet up on the coffee table, invite your thoughts and worries, and speak your mind. Perhaps you don't even *know* anymore what you want to fret about. If all else fails? Start ranting. Your only job until that timer goes off is to focus on your worries. As in a good brainstorming session, there are no rules: You don't have to select your thoughts; there are no "yes, buts," judgments, or practical objections. Just worry away!

Let your thoughts run wild like a mob of feral horses, sweating and untamed. Revel in your own misery like never before. Perhaps you'll have a revelation. Perhaps you'll have an epiphany or a glimpse of a solution. Or maybe not. When the timer goes off, stop. If necessary, schedule a new time to vent, but hold yourself to that time limit.

You'll discover at least two things. First, that worries lose their intensity when you dedicate your full time and attention to them. This is how you deflate them. At some point, you'll be done. Worrying gets boring. If you listen carefully, you'll find you keep thinking the same thing over and over. If you ignore your worries, they'll keep demanding attention, but if you *do* listen to them, sooner or later you'll realize: Well, now I know. Boring!

Second, scheduling your rumination will save you energy. It's unnecessary to freak out about a difficult conversation while you're dancing at a music festival. You'd rather not be worrying if the person is angry at you while looking for your bike keys. Can you do anything to change things right this second? No? Then save your worrying for a better time.

Your brain is a work in progress. You can lay down new thought paths and neglect others. The more you work to circumvent your usual worry triggers, the more chance you have of curing your anxiousness. Everyday triggers can be things like social media, reading through text conversations with your ex, seeing those slacks that no longer fit or the inbox that you'll never be able to clear. Save yourself from all that.

Ask Yourself the Question

◇◇◇◇◇◇◇◇◇◇◇◇

Whenever I find myself in a worry mode while I really am, or would like to be, busy with something else, such as when I'm waiting in line at a cash register or watching a movie, I ask myself the Question: "What can I do about it *now*?" If the answer is "not a lot, really," then I hit the brakes. At most, I might write a quick note on my phone: E-mail this person, do this or that this week, try to find out more tomorrow, etc. I often feel relieved after asking myself the Question. It's as if you have a helicopter view of the layout of your own thoughts and can tackle the gridlock in one go. You possess this power.

// The Flowers of Tomorrow Are in the Seeds of Today

Be mindful of your habits and patterns

Rest, cleanliness, routine. Dutch parents swear by these rules of thumb, and for good reason: That classic trio is a balm for bad days and a foundation for better ones. Routine gives rhythm to your days and stops you from wasting time by weighing the same decisions day in and day out. Everyday life is full of recurring patterns and habits, and fortunately so: It would be exhausting *not* to have them. Did you know that there's a limited amount of decision making and a finite supply of self-control we have at our disposal on any given day? You can run out of these resources.

Your brain is happy with every routine action that saves you a decision. The only catch is that you will glide through the days so routinely that, although you may have taken care of the what and the how, you have forgotten the why.

Routines can benefit you, but they can also work against you. Are you still aware of which patterns and habits benefit you and which ones are mostly an energy drain? It's fascinating to investigate the root system undergirding your daily routine and to understand what feeds it. Which routines contribute to who you want to be and how you want to live, and which ones are stealthily doing the exact opposite? Which habits stem from self-care, love, efficiency, or a higher purpose? Which habits are the result of fear, loss of control, or emptiness?

Like everybody else, I have my ingrained ways. My autopilot takes over, and I fall back too easily on habits of which I'm no longer even aware. All my life I have, for example, been the president, treasurer, and secretary of the Order of the Guardians of Harmony. If there's any discomfort or imbalance in a group, I will work hard to restore harmony. It's a pattern that I've come to recognize in myself, and now I can gently call myself out on it: Hey, Eveline, this isn't your responsibility. Just let it go.

I've also amassed a vast collection of habits that don't particularly harm me, although they don't benefit me either: snoozing, procrastinating, and hoarding, to name but a few. They don't really amount to anything in particular; neither do they promote true relaxation, by the way. But, well, it's so comfortable not to contemplate your actions. Everything that can

EVELINE HELMINK

pass for business as usual means less work for the brain. Just tune out and go.

That's too bad, because patterns (how we react) and habits (what we do) often are so commonplace and ingrained that, to a large extent, they determine our reality. Through the sum of all these smaller and larger actions, we create the world around us. Gretchen Rubin wrote about the relationship between happiness and habits in her book *Better Than Before: Mastering the Habits of Our Everyday Lives.* She argues that 40 percent of our day is determined by habits and that most of those habits were formed and defined long ago. Think about your routine of going to work in the morning or visiting your parents on a Sunday. You follow these routines without giving them much thought.

Rubin's book is a call for careful consideration of which habits you'd like to have, and she argues in favor of consciously choosing certain habits instead of falling into them by chance or copying them from people who you think have their lives in order. "Copying other people's routines won't make us more creative or productive, even if these are the routines of geniuses; we should first learn our own nature and the habits that come with it," Rubin argues. So developing a set of routines that really suit you and that will do something positive for you requires more than just clever copying and pasting.

Changing a habit isn't easy. No matter how many practical tips and to-do lists you may find online, in practice the gap between knowing and doing is a thousand times wider than on paper.

Inspired by a lecture or a book, I've so often sworn a solemn oath that from now on I'd start doing everything differently, only to, slowly but surely, slide back into my old ways, in my head and in my life. I still haven't managed to routinely prepare myself a super healthy meal for the next day. I still don't take cold showers. I still don't do my workout in the morning just to get it out of the way.

I have, however, come across a few interesting and helpful eye-openers. First, it's good to know that you can train willpower, like a muscle. Through practice, you can build up and strengthen the discipline needed to change yourself—so it really does make sense to start.

Another helpful activity for bad days is trying to understand *why* you do what you do. A habit or a pattern that doesn't really serve you (anymore) doesn't need to be broken in a dramatic and sweeping fashion; sometimes it's smarter to think or write for a while about a habit you have, to interrogate and understand it, instead of wanting to change it immediately. Get to know yourself first. That way, you aren't only fighting symptoms, but also discovering their cause.

Old habits can keep you trapped in unsatisfying patterns in your life, but establishing a routine can also have the opposite result: It can set you in motion. What helps me, if I want to add a new habit to my daily schedule, is connecting it to a bigger picture, making it part of a narrative. What is greater than this moment alone? What is the underlying value, the future dream, the long-term objective? All the flowers of all the tomorrows are in the seeds of today. What flowers am I hoping will bloom?

Exercising, meditating, changing the way you eat, or reorganizing your days because "they" say it's good for you is counterproductive. Like the yogi Vivekananda said: "Your path is good for you, but not for me. My path is good for me, but not for you." The manifesting energy for truly changing your life always comes from within. You plant the seeds deep inside yourself.

There are various opinions about how long it takes to master a new habit. Some say twenty-one days, others thirty. Another figure you'll often hear is ninety days. I would say it takes as long as it takes. Don't fool yourself with deadlines; they will only prove frustrating. You either want to change something or you don't. Something is going to increasingly give you energy or increasingly cost you energy.

I personally like to have a visual reminder of progress. Sometimes I hang a tape measure on my refrigerator. Every day that I manage to live up to a resolution, I cut off an inch. This keeps me occupied for about sixty days, if not longer. I used a measuring tape to represent the deadline for this book. It reminded me to keep moving forward and to not waste time with endless doubts. Inch by inch, day after day. And as you can see, the book got finished in the end. Don't expect that if you start exercising today, you will be fit tomorrow. Clear out one drawer; you don't have to do the whole cabinet right away. Remember: A turtle might be slow, but it will eventually get to where it needs to be.

The Art of Kaizen

◇◇◇◇◇◇◇◇◇◇◇◇

There is a Japanese philosophy called *kaizen* in which the path to change consists of teeny-tiny baby steps. A minute of meditation. Getting up five minutes earlier. One half glass less of soda. The only requirement is that you do it with love and dedication. The result is the payoff and not an end in itself. It's not a project; it's about the process. The trick is to enjoy what you find important and remain patient. Sometimes just visualizing what you want to achieve is already a first step in the right direction—after all, never underestimate the power of good intentions. Kaizen light is ideal for lesser days—especially the idea that a small change is better than no change. After all, watching Netflix for two hours is already a lot more wholesome than spending the entire day glued to your screen. And a glass of wine is still less than a whole bottle.

Baby steps!

// Let's Talk about Beyoncé for a Minute

Mapping who you are

"I just am who I am." It has always been difficult for me to relate to that sentence. It sounds so firm, so rigid and set in stone. My "self" today isn't the same as it was yesterday or five years ago, let alone ten years ago. And then there's the "self." Wise philosophers, spiritual teachers, and artists all more or less agree that that is a tough cookie. It seems to be there, but as soon as you want to grab it, define it, or make it tangible, it appears elusive. So much has been written and said about the "I" and the "self" that studying this topic could keep you off the streets for decades.

Those who continue to pursue a spiritual path will, at some point, be taught that everything you think is an illusion, a construction of experiences and feelings and thoughts that you have come to believe in. A metaphor for this construction is that of the movie, the projector, and the light. The movie is the narrative, in which you are playing a role. As spectators, we're sitting on the red velvet, completely absorbed by the screenplay on the big silver screen. So realistic! So compelling!

The moment you are able to detach yourself from the screen, you realize that the movie is a projection. Among other things, meditation is a way to become aware of this: The movie you see is a projection of the film containing your own experiences, patterns, desires, and fears.

But what about the self? The ego is neither the screen nor the film strip; it isn't even the projector. The self is the bright light shining through the projector. A beautiful metaphor: Your true self is the source of everything. You could also call the self by other names—"light" or "love." Others call it "consciousness," "the true self," or "your frequency." On bad days, the light of that true "self" still shines just as bright; you're just watching a more mediocre movie, nothing more. This image puts things in perspective, doesn't it?

Now, let's talk about Beyoncé. Or, actually, about Sasha Fierce. Sasha has been Bey's stage alter ego for many years. In 2008, she released a double album; one disc was titled *I Am* and mainly contained ballads; the other was titled *Sasha Fierce*. That disc contained her power songs, including the super famous "Single Ladies." The message was that there's a confident, sensual, and radiant Beyoncé and a calm, soft Beyoncé, and both sides got their moment to shine.

Sasha Fierce was the character that Beyoncé used when performing onstage: that side gave her energy, a role to fully inhabit, in all its glitter and glamour. At the same time, Beyoncé wanted to make mature, intimate music that was not just powerful but vulnerable. She wanted both. And why not? I remember that when that album came out, I thought the whole idea was brilliant: Don't see your apparent contradictions as undesirable, unclear, or confusing. Acknowledge them and play with them. Knowing and showing yourself completely—that seems to me to be one of the greatest gifts you can give yourself.

Knowing who you are makes things easier. Not knowing who you are makes things more complicated. It's that simple.

That unshakable "I am who I am" is no longer an armor, but something you can let go, allow to flow freely, a concept you can work with. In some respect, we are cut diamonds; which facet lights up depends on how the light hits us. In the summer of 2018, couple and family therapist Esther Perel was a guest on *Zomergasten*, a renowned long-form interview show on Dutch public television. One of her statements was, "Sometimes you need many people to get to know one person." She meant that we invariably show different aspects of the same self in different situations. That's who we are. We are all double albums. At least.

Do you know all your various selves? When I first got a position as editorial director, I was very young. I took part in intensive leadership training in which we were asked to map our "selves." One of the exercises was to portray as many sides of yourself as possible on a large sheet containing empty ovals. To get started, I dutifully began to draw: daughter, girlfriend, journalist, editorial director, et cetera. I made quite some strides. But after that, I kept drawing. It's such a simple exercise, but at the same time such an enlightening one. Among other versions, I drew my restless self, and the prankster, the consoler, the catty me, the ambitious me, the connector, the lazy-body, the listener, the introvert, the calm me, the extrovert, the daydreamer, the mule, the melancholic, the flirt, the hippie, the realist, the ponderer, the romantic.

Sound familiar? Sometimes you want to dance, sometimes you want to lounge on the sofa. Sometimes you are swearing and cursing, sometimes you keep it bottled up. Sometimes you sport red lipstick, sometimes you prefer not to stand out. Sometimes you are Sasha, sometimes you are Beyoncé. You contain multitudes.

Feel free to play with your identity, and don't let others restrict you. Make a list for yourself. You don't need to share that list with anyone; it's meant just for you. It helps you see which self will step up in which situation. It will also help you to consider whether you actually need that particular self in a certain moment.

Remember this: Each of your sides, the beautiful ones and their less flattering peers, ultimately derive from the same source. Your grumpy, catty, and unreasonable selves belong just as much as your more attractive selves. Not infrequently, their intentions are good. They just want to protect you from disappointment or pain, even if they do so clumsily or even unconsciously. If you are aware of all your selves, it becomes easier to take a step back, allowing another self to step forward. It can make a world of difference, especially on lesser days. "Ah, there is my melodramatic self. Maybe she should make way for my optimistic self." You carry them all inside you. To quote Thich Nhat Hanh: "You recognize it, you smile at it, and you invite something kinder to come forward and take its place."

Being true to yourself is not the same as being unchangeable. Being true to yourself is seeing yourself as one instrument, with many sounds.

And sometimes you have to shut up the cacophony of your selves, to silence the instrument. Deep inside, you often know exactly—without roles or masks—what you need.

EVELINE HELMINK

// Laugh about It

Humor as a coping mechanism

In the early spring of 2018, despite informal care and support, my mother was no longer able to live at home and was permanently admitted to a nursing home for people with early-onset dementia, where she now lives. In the days leading up to the move, my brothers and I were busy making her room as comfortable as possible. With my brother Matthijs, I drove to Ikea for the final purchases. Normally, we would have a lot of fun in such a place—trying out the beds, racing carts through the warehouse—but when you are picking out pillows for your sick mother for a house that is not her home, Ikea suddenly becomes a strange environment. We went to the checkout and paid.

Dementia is an ugly disease. It makes you forget who and where you are. As we packed our purchases, my brother tapped me on the shoulder and pointed to a text that was glued to the wall in large block letters. "Everyone forgets something sometime," it said, hanging over the screws and bolts. "Everyone forgets something sometime . . ." A comforting message from Ikea. It made us laugh so hard.

I don't know anything better than humor as a ready-made way to breathe some air into situations that feel heavy and solid. Quite literally! Laughing causes you to take a deep breath. Laughter isn't to everyone's taste: I can remember situations in which my chuckle might have been a little off the mark, but I simply couldn't help myself. No matter how heavy, how sad or desperate the moment, sooner or later there'll be a joke ripe for the making. Make it. It puts things in perspective.

Your body is happy with laughter. When you laugh, the number of antibodies in your saliva increases, your muscles relax, your blood pressure drops, you produce endorphins that work as an analgesic. All very welcome on bad days. Even when you just grimace, like putting on a faux smile for an ill-fated selfie attempt, it's almost impossible to have negative thoughts. Fake laughter has almost the same effect on your body as real laughter. You can even do laughter workouts that teach you to experience the biological benefits of pleasure. What works even better than intentional exercises to experience the therapeutic effect of the smile is, of course, real laughter, so crack some jokes.

For some, serious spiritual exercise and humor don't mix well. The prevailing theory seems to be that you need a deadly serious look on your face when you're meditating and are tuned in to divine frequencies. Perhaps we believe that a serious face yields serious insights? However, if you ignore that there are also things that you should *not* take too gravely, you aren't living inclusively. Your own thoughts, for instance. Self-mockery is a form of ego-lessness and putting yourself in perspective. In Eastern religions, humor is generally more appreciated; both on the meditation mat and in teaching, laughter is seen as a perfect way to get out of the mind and into the moment. There are many Buddhist jokes, riddles, and parables that make fun of the ego.

The moment you start taking yourself too seriously, you are missing the ability to really connect. If you ask me, the ability to observe yourself from the outside is essential for personal growth. Humor pushes you out of your personal territory and invites you to try a different perspective. At spiritual teachings or yoga classes in which the rooms are filled with rolling laughter, you can almost feel the energy in the space opening up and relaxation setting in. There is a time for silence and attention, just as there's a time for liberation and expression. In modern spirituality, when reactions to humor can be touchy in general, it's important to remember its power. Breathing some lightness into everyday life is anything but frivolous; it is a highway to light and air. A heartfelt smile is very honest.

Taking everything seriously actually is an ego thing, because it ignores the fact that we create our own reality. Life can be seen as one big cosmic joke. To quote the poet Robert Frost: "Forgive, o Lord, my little jokes on Thee, and I will forgive Thy great big one on me."

According to American psychologist Harvey Mindess, you can see humor like this: It pokes fun at all those layers around our soul with which we identify ourselves, such as status, appearances, and possessions. It peels off all those layers and brings us into contact with what remains: the soul. Learning to laugh at life and at yourself is a great way to get rid of all that is rigid and troublesome. And the ego actually benefits from a little contradiction. The ability to see the humor in something can lead you, in a direct and immediate way, to new insights, an unexpected solution, or a new conversation.

// There's Nothing Wrong with Saying "Yes, But..."

Some "Yes, buts" are soulguards

A good friend once told me about one of his favorite Star Wars scenes. In *The Empire Strikes Back*, Yoda tells Luke Skywalker to lift a spaceship out of a swampy lake, but he complains that it's very heavy. The job, he says, is of a different caliber than moving a stone. To which Yoda says, "No. No different. Only different in your mind. You must unlearn what you have learned."

Luke replies: "Oh, all right, I'll give it a try." Yoda counters, "No. Try not. Do or do not. There is no try."

No "Yes, buts" for Luke. Yes or no, with nothing in between. I found the scene rather odd. Black-and-white thinking is quite common in modern life. Expressing doubt isn't sexy. You know what you want, right? If you aren't sure, it's definitely not going to work! But actually, it's weird, this idea that you aren't allowed to have any objections to your own or other people's thoughts. If your "yes, but" stems from fear of failure, then sure, Yoda might be a little right. "Yes, buts" that arise from fear are standing between life and you.

You probably know this feeling: You want to pass someone, and they jokingly step in front of you to block your way. If you then take a step to the right, the other person also steps to the right. This is a game that quickly gets annoying. "Yes, buts" can be similar: They put up roadblocks that prevent you from moving on. "Yes, but I can't do this" and "Yes, but it's not the right time" put a brake on your creativity, your space, and your growth.

But to dismiss all "yes, buts" as signs of weakness would be a shame. "Yes, buts" are also mirrors: You can see yourself crystal clear in them. There are "yes, buts" you can use as a shield, off which everything ricochets—"yes, but you," "yes, but life." There are also useful "yes, buts"—those that remind you of the steps you've forgotten along the way, warning you of naivety, drowsiness, or just carelessness. "Yes, but maybe this is not what I need right now." "Yes, but you are now making me do your emotional labor." There are plenty of very sympathetic "yes, buts" that do not intend to block your way at all, but rather prevent you from falling into a trap. These "yes, buts" are like bodyguards, soulguards. A well-intentioned "yes, but" on a bad day isn't necessarily a cop-out. So by all means, go for it: "yes, but" away.

// Gratitude Feels Good

What millennial pink is to Instagram and a flat white is to a hipper-than-thou coffee shop, gratitude is to a lighter, more present life, which is to say it's ubiquitous. The sun rising, a fresh cup of tea—you can take it all for granted, but you can also choose to be thankful for it. Considering what you have received makes you feel good, or at least makes you feel slightly better on a bad day. No matter how cranky you are, no matter how dreadful the days, there is always *something* to think of. The simple fact that you have hot and cold running water. That spring will always return, whether you like it or not. That there is such a thing as Carpool Karaoke. It doesn't have to be something epic like Love or Life. Even seeing a unicorn on a mug, finding a feather, or spontaneously catching the moment that 12:34 p.m. lights up on your phone can be cause for one nanosecond of positivity, a spark of "Hey, that's kinda nice, or funny, or lovely" in even the grumpiest of minds.

What's striking is that, these days, gratitude seems to have caught on. Even the most down-to-earth, pragmatic humans seem to see the benefits of gratitude as a tool for a lighter life; they write books about it and apply it to less obvious settings, such as boardrooms. Maybe it's partly because "gratitude" sounds soft, but it's anything but; there is hard scientific evidence that a grateful attitude to life is a good idea. People who pay attention to what goes on in their lives and reflect on what they find valuable earn reward points toward many interesting things: a stronger immune system, the experience of more positive feelings, more confidence, meaning, energy, and a better sleep cycle, just to name a few.

If you have taught yourself to keep track of what you are grateful for, this lesson will augment your everyday experiences. Things become less obvious or less random. Not only is gratitude suitable for days when everything goes well (it keeps your focus on what matters), but even if you think there is little to be thankful for, you will discover that there is always a bright spot, if you look closely.

The term "gratitude" has suffered a bit from how we dealt with it in previous eras. Whole generations have grown up with obligatory gratitude. Because they hadn't lived through World War II. Because God demanded it. Because there are starving children in Africa.

Another question arises: Who exactly should we thank? That's up to you, but if you don't experience God or another higher power, you can still be thankful that you receive anything at all from life itself. Here on earth, we are totally dependent on nature and on each other, from the plants that provide us with oxygen to the water that makes life possible to our mothers who carried us. "Life is a game of give-and-take," as you've probably heard someone say in a lecture. There's a lot of truth in that, because we give and receive—from God, the universe, or providence.

Gratitude is a nice feeling. I love it when it just happens to be there. I call it a "radiant heart," that swelling, warm feeling in my chest that can overwhelm me. It can also be a lump in my throat or an almost imperceptible skipped heartbeat. Grateful moments are like fireflies: They are particularly magical in the darkness.

Starting a Gratitude Journal
When Things Feel Shitty

◇◇◇◇◇◇◇◇◇◇◇◇◇◇

Don't overthink that perfect first sentence in your pristine, gold-imprinted notebook of handmade paper. Just put your pen to paper. Break the blank. And if those perfect, virgin pages deter you from writing, just grab a sticky note or scribble on the back of a used envelope.

There is no jury looking over your shoulder. Do not dutifully record what you think you *should* be grateful for. Write down what you *actually* feel grateful for. No judgment. Focus on what brings you a radiant heart and not on what is socially acceptable or spiritually desirable. Sometimes you may feel gratitude for a beautiful sunset or a great yoga class, but sometimes you may really be more grateful that you found some forgotten candy under the seat of your car.

Don't just focus on things. It is obvious to first look at what you have in a material sense: a gift received, a bed, a house. But you can also think, for example, of experiences, of opportunities that came along, or of something sensory, such as a smell, a sound, or a taste. Last but not least, consider the people around you. What happens between them and you can also be of value: advice, a tip, an insight, a good joke.

Don't just note the "what," but also the "why." Why are you thankful for it?

Be grateful for what flows in from the outside and what comes to you, but also for what flows out of you: You can be grateful for what you were able to contribute, create, or achieve.

You can apply a kind of abs workout schedule to gratitude: first three gratitude crunches a day, then five, then ten. Practice, and build it up. Quality over quantity: Can you really only think of one thing? Then that's good enough for that moment.

Your journal doesn't necessarily have to be writing. Include pictures, concert tickets, drawings; even just dashes for every time you feel gratitude can suffice as well. Moments can be captured in many ways.

Choose a fixed time for your experiment. If you do, it's more likely to become a routine. Bedtime is often a favorite moment, sort of like backing up the day's body, mind, and soul data.

// Long Live Boredom

Feeling bored doesn't have to be so bad

As a child, I spent endless hours lying down and listening to the large clock in our living room. You could literally hear time passing. I knew how to enjoy myself, but I could also be bored out of my mind. I remember watching the shadows on the wall, the grain of our wooden coffee table, and the homey smell of the fabric upholstery of our sofa. I'd listen to the sounds from in and around the house: the rustling of a newspaper, the noise of clattering skateboards belonging to my brother and his friends on the street out front.

I easily could've gotten up and done something, but I didn't. Maybe I knew intuitively that being bored has its pleasant aspects. There was nothing that needed to be done and no place my presence was required. Today, I envy that girl with oceans of time to float around in. I always seem to have things that need doing or somewhere I need to be. Of course, to a certain extent this "having to" is a choice; nevertheless, at times I miss doing nothing.

I'm just not as good at being bored anymore. As an adult, you have so many fewer "in between" moments. Life forces itself into the days, hours, and minutes like spray foam. There are hardly any moments when you truly have nothing to do.

A delayed flight, a dentist's waiting room, a delivery guy not showing up: I savor these situations. The no-man's-land between now and soon is a gift of time. You could call it living in the moment, but I prefer to call it circumstantial mindfulness; you accidentally trip over the now.

Being bored is not the same as meditation or rest, activities for which you make time and on which you focus your attention. When you're bored, there seems to be nothing worth your attention, nothing that is giving you energy. We are living from one experience to the next. Being bored is standing still. You might want something exciting to happen, something that titillates you—but nope, life is tedious and uninteresting. It isn't necessarily a pleasant sensation; at times, it can feel more like being in a desert where the sun is shining down mercilessly. Without any distraction, without a fresh spring or area of shade to escape to, there is only what there is. And that can be inconvenient sometimes.

EVELINE HELMINK

Precisely because we live a life rich with sensory stimuli, a little boredom is actually good for us.

With some patience, what is empty can fill up with reflection, daydreaming, creativity, or the simple acceptance that there is only nothing. I mean, how often do you *really* feel that emptiness?

Boredom is an exercise. An exercise in being with what is there and being able to amuse yourself with nothing more than your own thoughts, desires, and imagination. Your brain wants to be stimulated; that is how it stays active and constantly forms new cells. That's how you automatically become curious and creative.

If you allow the boredom to be, you open the gates, as it were, between your consciousness and your subconsciousness, and you will hear your inner voice more clearly than if you allowed yourself some outside stimuli just so you didn't have to feel the boredom. A four-hour train delay, for example, can be just as interesting as a ten-minute dedicated meditation; when you're turned off, something is going on at a deeper level.

When you are having a bad day, allow boredom to happen. You will discover that if you will just relax, something will happen, if only something very small. There is now room for original thoughts; you get closer to yourself. Sometimes it can be nice to purposely provoke this state of mind. Why don't you go and sit on a random bench in a random street in a random neighborhood without any distractions (leave your phone at home!). Don't hang out at that hip coffee shop with the inspiring view. Find a place where nothing in particular stimulates you. Take a tour on a random city bus. "Nothing to do, nowhere to be, a simple little kind of free," John Mayer sang, which is nicely put.

The Bore-Out

◇◇◇◇◇◇◇◇◇◇◇◇◇◇◇◇

Strange but true: You can be totally unaware that you're bored. And just as you can be not bored enough, you can be too bored. Maybe you aren't having a lesser day because *something* has happened but because *nothing* is happening at all. A bore-out can be a problem as well, just like a burnout. You may recognize serious boredom via symptoms like this:

- *You derive less or no energy from the things you do.*
- *Meetings, to-dos, routines:* They weigh ever heavier and more like obligations, without feeling necessary.
- *You look for excuses to justify not doing what you're supposed to be doing.*
- *Your attention wanders in every direction; you're a little suspended above reality.*
- *You sleep more than you need.*
- *Your body feels heavy and sluggish.*

Recognize any of these? Take them seriously. This kind of boredom is like quicksand. It's time to take matters into your own hands and explore what you need to do to regain your energy. Treat the symptoms (go for a walk, go to the movies, stimulate your mind), but also address the cause. Investigate where your energy is draining from and what you need to feel stimulated again.

// Do the Savasana

This is the only yoga exercise in this book

I'm just going to tell it like it is: Performing the savasana pose is practicing being dead. It's also known as corpse pose because that's how you're lying there, like a corpse—on your back, no muscle tension, not doing anything at all. Except breathe, that is. You don't even need to put on your yoga pants or whip out a sports bra. All you need is your focus, your body, and a place to temporarily lay your body down on the floor. Sounds easy, right? Wrong. While the pose itself may not be difficult to assume, experts and loyal practitioners have called it one of the most difficult yoga exercises. Because even though you are lying on your back doing nothing, it can feel as if you're climbing Kilimanjaro, especially on a bad day. Total surrender and deep relaxation aren't easy.

It starts with your body. Slow down your breathing; thoroughly relax your muscles until you are comfortable and no longer feel the constant, restless urge to wobble and to rearrange your body; do not squeeze your eyelids but allow them to fall shut . . . that is step one.

The savasana is relief for a stressed body. Your heart rate drops, the tension leaves your muscles, and your body starts to focus on its primary tasks of feeding, cleansing, and healing.

Once you manage to truly relax, it will feel as if the earth is carrying you.

However, the savasana is also, and perhaps primarily, a mental exercise in surrender, in relaxation, in calming your monkey mind. It is not the time to go over your day and prepare your shopping list, not the time to hold on to your thoughts and impressions; it is time for allowing them to freely flutter, without an active response.

There are no other yoga poses in this book because I myself am not a yogi. Yoga can do a lot for us, and if it appeals to you, it is certainly a practice worth investigating. For the savasana, I made an exception because this is the pose that has made the difference more than once in times when I didn't know what to do with myself. As a cheerleader of allowing emotions to flow and examining life's reality, I stubbornly sought ways to make that work during the period right after I got divorced. Below the surface, I felt all sorts of emotions bubbling. Often, however, I failed to break through my self-preservation armor. It was like a pimple that was already pushing and nagging underneath my skin, but couldn't be popped yet. But whenever I lay in the savasana position, fully surrendering myself, when my tight muscles relaxed, something deep inside saw its chance, and tears rolled down my cheeks. I went through that calmly, without judgment, surrendering to what apparently had to move. It was a release of negative energy. That's how I let go.

Pema Chödrön rightly reminds us that we grow up in a culture that fears death and hides it. But death is all around us (we'll talk about that more on p. 99). Chödrön writes about everyday dying: "We experience it in the form of disappointment, in the form of things that don't work out the way we wanted. We experience it in the form of things perpetually being in a state of flux. When the day ends, when a second ends, when we breathe out, that is dying in everyday life."

There's a reason savasana is known as corpse pose: Each time you let go of an earthly trepidation, you die a little. Everything that lives arises from what has died before—life and death are inextricably linked. When you let go, something new will take its place. Trust this process.

You die a little bit when you give your ego a time-out. You die a little, because you leave the world for what it is. It's a goodbye. And then? Where do we go from there? A restart. A reset. Isn't that exactly what you need on a bad day? A chance to start over, lighter, more carefree, if with only one grain of sand less heaviness in your heart.

How to Do a Savasana

✧✧✧✧✧✧✧✧✧✧✧

On a lesser day, you can make the exercise as complicated or as easy as you like. Put on a yoga outfit and grab a mat and a blanket if you feel like it. You may also plop down on the floor in the office mail room in whatever you are wearing—it's all good.

1. Ideally you create a cocoon: the light slightly dimmed, warmth provided by a blanket or a well-heated room, maybe some soft music. But a cocoon is not a requirement. Fluorescent lights you can't shut off? It is what it is.

2. Make yourself comfortable. You may want something to support your head or the back of your knees; if you don't have a pillow handy, it could just as well be your bag or a rolled-up vest.

3. Place your feet hip-width apart, heels loosely on the floor, and let your feet relax; usually they will fall to the side slightly, toes pointing out. Place your arms at your sides with your palms up.

4. Deeply breathe in and out. If necessary, do it theatrically: Take in a deep breath and exhale with a "ffffffff" sound. Try to release a little more tension from your body with each breath. Fake it until you make it, but breathe naturally. Forcing your breathing to slow down won't work; calm your breath diligently but gradually.

5. Focus your attention on your body. Direct your mind from your toes all the way to your crown, without skipping a single part—each toe, the soles of your feet, your heels, your ankles, and so on. Guide your breath to wherever you feel restless.

6. Observe your thoughts in a calm manner. It's impossible to stop thinking entirely. By the time you're out of thoughts, you're no longer in the land of the living. You can rise above your thoughts, however, by returning to a center, a point of attention. Visualize a pleasant place, as some sort of screensaver for your soul that you can always return to.

7. Allow emotions to flow without letting them carry you away. Observe them. Keep calm and always try to find the center, letting yourself be guided by your breathing.

8. After about twenty minutes, slowly start moving again by wiggling, moving, and getting active. You may also stay a little longer; this is your exercise, after all. But if you notice that your anxiety is increasing, cut the exercise short and try again later.

// Take Your Alone Time

You could safely lock me up in my house for a month and I'd be completely content. Secretly, I'm a hermit; I really enjoy being alone. As long as I have something to read, something to listen to, and something to eat, I'll enjoy myself and often will even be happy. "Yes, easily said, if you also have a rich social life," observed a critical friend. She argued that being alone by choice and being alone due to circumstances are two entirely different things. And that's true. Being lonely is also different from being alone. Loneliness has no counterbalance; the equilibrium has been disrupted. Being alone, as a choice, is about something else.

Receiving only external energy and stimuli will throw you off balance. You also need to have space to feel the stimuli coming from inside.

Imbalance is fertile ground for bad days. Often I have less attention to share than is asked of me. Working full-time in a busy editorial office, I need to attend to press events and lectures and deadlines and friends and family and children and dentists, soccer practice, hairdressers, dinner parties, reunions, parent-teacher meetings, sports classes, and overtime, and it's a never-ending grind. If I didn't consciously choose to be alone every now and then, it would hardly ever happen.

Taking time for yourself isn't always socially accepted. For example, my friends like to drag me out of my house because "What else am I going to do anyway?" And saying no to an appointment with a friend or for business because you want to say yes to an appointment with yourself remains difficult to explain sometimes; you have to be on the verge of a burnout if you want to be able to cancel for reasons like "me time" or "alone time." I challenge you to do so anyway.

In her book *Women Who Run with the Wolves*, Clarissa Pinkola Estés writes: "Long ago, the word 'alone' was treated as two words. All one. To be all one meant to be wholly one, to be in oneness, either essentially or temporarily. That's precisely the goal of solitude, to be all one." It can be beneficial to isolate yourself. It removes all noise and brings you close to yourself. You can hear yourself think for a moment. I find that nothing is as nice as walking through a strange city or along a strange beach all by myself, anonymous and out of place. It gives me space to organize my thoughts, attune myself to my pure desires and needs, and become aware of the signals my body or mind want to give me.

50

Sometimes that leads to profound philosophical thoughts—and sometimes it leads to nothing special, except a deep sense of freedom. Time you spend with yourself is an opportunity to recharge. Even if you take fifteen minutes a day for yourself—taking a walk or sitting down by yourself—you will see that it brings you closer to that source.

I also like to start my working days on my own. I prefer to be at home for the first half hour to an hour, doing what I think is important, finding out what I'm going to focus on that day before I "hand myself over" and connect. Another favorite: going to the movies alone. You don't need company there, in the dark, in silence. Nothing beats being absorbed by a story and afterward riding your bike home, alone with your own thoughts, without other people's opinions or noise. Being comfortable with just yourself and being comfortable with others in equal measure is very important to me when it comes to personal growth and a meaningful life.

Spirituality is often about receiving energy, but it is just as important to shut yourself off from energy. For example, I am hypersensitive to sensory stimuli when it comes to sound. In a restaurant, I follow ten conversations at the same time, I hear ticking and murmuring and squeaking along with everything else. I remember putting on headphones with active noise cancellation for the first time in Los Angeles. It was as if I'd seen the light. "I will never have to hear other people ever again!" I said euphorically to the boy in his Apple shirt, who frowned. But I didn't mean it that way: I loved and love that I have the choice to be with my own thoughts, even if I can't isolate myself in a literal sense.

Finally, and this does not officially count as a shortcut unless you are now about to board a train or a plane, but I highly recommend traveling alone at least once—experiencing a strange environment, relying only on your own senses, beliefs, emotions, and thoughts for navigation. It has given me a strong foundation to discover that I can be in my own company and be perfectly fine. It strengthens your confidence in your own voice, and leads to deeper self-knowledge and a more pure contact with your intuition. This seems to happen faster and more intensely especially when you are in an unfamiliar environment. Whether it was a week in Melbourne in my twenties, or a trip across Iceland, or more recently wandering around Tokyo or spending a period in Los Angeles to write—I found it all equally inspiring and cathartic.

And yes, traveling solo can be uncomfortable. There is a kind of social stigma attached to it: Didn't you have anyone to come along with you? It can be awkward to sit in a restaurant all by yourself. You have to know how to handle it. As I wrote before, this is mostly due to the confusion between "being alone" and "being lonely." It is the difference between balance and imbalance in your inner world.

I also love to travel with others, which is very intimate and has a different vibe. But comparing the two modes of travel goes beyond the point I'm trying to make, that there are some very valuable aspects of traveling alone, including meeting new people who will allow you to show yourself as you are, without submitting to a single assumption or projection. Traveling on your own strips you of the layer of social dust that everyone collects, willingly or unwillingly.

Solo adventures work like a kind of soul-Swiffer: An encounter in a new environment, in a new context, can sweep your original self clean again.

Another valuable part of the experience is learning how to entertain, comfort, help, and guide yourself. You can't just shuffle along behind your traveling companions, half lost in thought; you need to be more alert and attentive to your environment. Your senses become more "awake": You taste your food more vividly if you are not distracted by a conversation; the water feels different when you finally decide to take a dip; you hear the morning sounds clearly when no one is snoring. Maybe traveling by yourself to a far destination isn't your cup of tea, but there's always just a night in a new city. Give it a try.

I Have a Garden in My Heart

◇◇◇◇◇◇◇◇◇◇

I can identify with a quote from Cheryl Strayed about being alone. She writes, "Alone had always felt like an actual place to me, as if it weren't a state of being, but rather a room where I could retreat to be who I really was." There are many names for that place deep within you, where there is no judgment, no time, and no pain. Your quiet space, some teachers call it. Or your sacred space. However cheesy, I myself prefer the term "the garden in my heart." I like that image; I picture a walled, overgrown English garden, with wild flowers, knotted trees, and tall grass in which you can lie down and look at a clear blue sky. On hard days, it's gratifying to imagine such a place, because sometimes an image can help you quickly reach a place inside yourself where you can be alone, even when, in fact, you are not.

// **Just Sit with the Pain**

On sitting out the storm and soul combing

Sometimes a bad day can hit you like a sudden thunderstorm, lightning and all. Life has a habit of flooding you without warning, almost unbearably so. At times, I have fervently wished that the earth would split open and swallow me up, just so that the bad day would stop, immediately. For those moments, I have a simple mantra: Sit with the pain. Like during a storm, when you have nowhere else to go, you just have to wait it out, as if you were snowed in by your own emotions.

Keep breathing and feeling: only that. Sometimes I feel the thunder in every fiber in my body, and I just sit with the pain, while I breathe calmly and deeply. Because there is no other option. And with every breath I try to stay present. Not because it is comfortable: On the contrary, it is super uncomfortable. This is *not* a fun exercise. But I know I will regret it later when I don't do it. There is no point in numbing or hiding pain. Hiding fresh pain is the same as hiding fresh fish: Sooner or later, you'll find out it's a really bad idea.

So, sit with the pain. Sometimes, on a bad day, that's really all that needs to be done. Give yourself your full attention. Feel your feelings. Recently, I was caught by a wave of anger and embarrassment, one of my least favorite emotional cocktails. It hit and seared my body: My cheeks were hot, and it felt like lava was pouring into my chest. In the meantime, I started doing the dishes, just to kill some time. Giving your hands a nice shame-filled soak in soapy water. What else can you do? The pain is there.

Sitting out the storm means letting your emotions run their course. And I've come to learn that I can rely on the following idea: The pain will pass, just as rain will pass and snow will melt. After the storm peaks and the wind and rain ease off, things get brighter, safer. And although a few roof tiles have blown off and a branch has fallen, the house and the tree are still standing. The time has come to see how things should proceed, but the worst is over.

// A Little Discipline

But do it only for yourself

It is unfortunate but true: Discipline doesn't come naturally to me. I do have perseverance. If something makes my heart beat faster, I will work dutifully, diligently to the bitter end. But if I don't immediately see the purpose of something . . . well, sometimes I have to dig deep, very deep, to stay motivated. I envy people who have an iron discipline. Take the father of my children; he has it in spades. The moment he sets his sights on something, he turns it into a project and devotedly applies himself. For example, he earned an MBA the year our first son was born. He combined completing an intensive yoga teacher training with a full-time job and taught himself to play the guitar via YouTube. When we were together, that sometimes was a point of contention; the more fanatically he rolled out his yoga mat in the morning and did his asanas, the more fanatically I avoided the whole practice. Still, for a meaningful life, discipline is pretty useful. Meditation, attention, self-examination—the discipline for these doesn't come easy.

Discipline requires practice and dedication. It means taking responsibility for yourself and the life you want to lead.

Sometimes I waste precious time painting my nails, checking Instagram, organizing books by color, and shuffling my furniture around when I could be doing something different, bigger, more important. Lacking discipline on a bad day feels horrible, because especially then you need some semblance of willpower to move toward the light. The great thing is that you can train yourself to have willpower and discipline—literally. You can control the part of your brain where willpower resides, activating it through practice. This is good news, because that makes it very worthwhile to give it a try. Without any discipline, after all, you continue to act based on what you already know and are familiar with, and doing so means you'll never get ahead.

The secret of healthy discipline is making sure it's balanced energy-wise. You want an adequate return on your investment. When you are solely driven by your ego—you worry about what others will think if you don't work out enough or fail to meet a deadline—discipline will often end up costing you more than it yields. Your relaxation, your social life, or your mental health may suffer, to name but a few aspects of life where discipline is valuable. Staying disciplined isn't a donation box for the approval, admiration, and appreciation of the people around you. Healthy discipline gives you a sense of self-worth, a goal, satisfaction.

What helps me to stay disciplined is a combination of ownership, self-compassion, higher purpose, and trust. In other words, I make conscious choices, and I am willing—to put in work, for example, or to forgo things. I forgive myself when I fail, and I investigate the reasons I failed. I find out why I do what I do, and I formulate a long-term goal and know why taking action is important to me. I trust that when I stray, I can always return and that, eventually, I'll end up where I want to be, in a way that works for me and at a time that works for me. On bad days, I no longer have to doubt that.

// **Stop Blaming Karma**

Karma is not "what goes around comes around" . . . then again, it actually kinda is. It's just a little more complicated and subtle than that.

On bad days, the concept of karma is often reduced to a worn-out term. It's mainly misinterpreted as a reservoir of negative feelings about punishment and justice and compensation. Take the karmic gun, the firing of negative vibes at others by making statements such as "Karma is a bitch"—the idea of "chickens coming home to roost" or "you will get what's coming to you." Maybe you have an arsenal of excuses, like "Karma made me do it." Another favorite is the classic karma complaining: What did I do to deserve this? All of this is giving karma a bad rep.

In Sanskrit, *karma* means something like "action" or "deed" and simply refers to the universal law of action and reaction. When you throw a pebble in the water, the surface ripples. Thus, every action, large or small, has a consequence. Negativity causes circles of negativity; positivity causes circles of positivity. That is a fact, no ulterior motive: no judgment, no punishment, and no reward. It is a pure observation of what is. Broadly speaking, you can see karma as follows: Your behavior today already carries the future with it. In all of your words, actions, and thoughts, you sow what is to come. Karma is not a court of judgment and punishment. It is simply the law of reciprocity.

For that precise reason, you yourself can change the direction of your karma. That makes it a powerful tool. When you manage to redirect your thoughts, by forgiving yourself or someone else or by feeling compassion for yourself or for others, you can balance so-called negative karma. When all your actions come from an intention of loving-kindness, karma doesn't come from the outside, but rather from the inside.

And, no, that doesn't mean there won't be any hassles or that other people will never annoy or hurt you again. At best, it means that you'll find the resilience and flexibility in yourself to deal with it better. When you are aware of your actions and motivations, you are creating something new for yourself. If you want a different result, you will have to take a different action. It's that simple.

If you aren't in the mood (yet) for self-reflection and just want to be angry or disappointed, then just leave karma out of it. Wielding karma as some sort of sword can quickly turn ugly. It may feel fair, but you may wonder who is eventually "learning a lesson." Feelings do want to be felt, but there isn't necessarily an effect or action associated with them. As much as we would like it, we often have no insight into the complexity of the cosmic fabric of which we are a single thread. Do what is right, and trust that the world at large will restore its balance without your personal interference.

Psychiatrist and Holocaust survivor Viktor Frankl, from whom we can learn quite a bit about resilience and justice, wisely said: "Between stimulus and response there is a space. In that space is our power to choose our response. In our response lies our growth and our freedom." Karma is no excuse for selling yourself or others short. Let it go. Karma is a matter of trust: If your acts are pure and loving, without expectations and without clumsiness, sooner or later you will reap the benefits.

// Loving-Kindness

Do you know what will really improve any bad day? What works universally and always and everywhere? Loving-kindness. Loving-kindness is the answer to everything.

The principle of loving-kindness stems from *metta*, which is what the Buddhist practice of gentleness and kindness is called. The Buddhist saint Guanyin—the name means something like "she who hears sounds of suffering in the world"—is the embodiment of this life skill. You may have seen an image of her: She has a thousand arms, and those arms are full of friendship, compassion, empathy, forgiveness, grace, and comfort. Guanyin has so many arms that she embraces everyone. And I mean really everyone: the schmucks, the criminals, those who are down on their luck, the ne'er-do-wells, even the people who don't feel they deserve that embrace.

Practicing loving-kindness isn't easy. On paper, it's beautiful; in practice, it can be difficult, especially if you are having a shitty day and actually feel the urge to give everyone who's bothering you a kick in the butt. On a bad day, someone bumping into my cart in the supermarket can be enough to tick me off.

Fortunately, loving-kindness is a quality you can develop, a skill you can learn, like riding a bike or tying your shoelaces. When loving-kindness becomes your basic attitude, everything in life becomes a little lighter. It is an effective cure against resentment, against shame, against a whole arsenal of negative emotions. By practicing loving-kindness, you develop compassion and empathy for yourself and others and for all the stupid things you do and they do.

After all, *metta* is also realizing that *everyone* has their particular flaws. Other people are also just doing whatever. And instead of snapping at them or pushing them away, perpetuating a vicious circle of crankiness in your mind, put your arm around them. For that matter, you can put an arm around yourself.

My *metta* hobby in a busy supermarket? Whenever there's a long line and the person behind me is sighing and groaning, I gracefully step aside and let them go first. It only costs me a couple of minutes that I can easily spare, and it invariably produces a smile. Just an everyday example of how simple acts of kindness can brighten your days.

While *metta* is something you can learn and develop, it's also innate. However cynical you may have become about the state of humanity from watching the news or observing the world around you, in essence we are loving, caring creatures. Really. We care. When you see someone hurting, isn't your first urge to offer your help? It is a primal instinct.

Today, for some incomprehensible reason, we have come to see kindness as a weakness, as if you are effacing yourself, as if you are submissive, as if you don't have anything better to do. After all, you are also busy and hurt and tired. People should take *that* into account for a change. These days, kindness often doesn't fit our needs. We prefer to make it through our days efficiently, unhindered, undisturbed.

Loving-kindness offers a different perspective: It is not at all about justifying or brushing away. It is about seeing what is there, perceiving, without directly attaching a judgment or action to it, and then thinking: What kind of wise, positive and loving contribution can I make?

It works both ways: People who practice loving-kindness are generally better at dealing with adversity. They are less downcast, because they feel there is always a choice, always an option that is positive and light.

Now, can I be loving and kind twenty-four seven? No. In an ideal world, we rise above our annoyances and setbacks. But we don't live in an ideal world. When riding my bike, I will still grumble about tourists casually walking in the bike lane. After a hard day, I'll blast Rage Against the Machine's "Killing in the Name" at full volume. All of that is present too, and we need to allow it, although by now I'm more inclined to keep it to myself.

Sometimes you have to move through negative energy to arrive at loving action. Anger, jealousy, and fear are often indicators of *metta*. They show where there's still friction and where there is room for improvement and relief.

What I do know: The more you practice loving-kindness, the easier it becomes to arrive at compassion. It's as if you were building a highway from your heart to your head, on which you can increasingly quickly travel the distance from cranky to friendly.

A *Metta* Exercise

◇◇◇◇◇◇◇◇◇◇

Calmly sit down and relax, making sure you are warm and comfortable, and close your eyes. Think of the person who is bothering you (or of yourself, if that's where you need to send some love) as a small child, open-minded, innocent, and vulnerable. Take this child on your lap and comfort it. Try to see both the child and yourself as imperfect, growing people, each with their own powerlessness and ineptitude. Doing so will breathe some air into feelings of revulsion or irritation. Behind all our masks and humanity, we are all made of the same stardust.

Create for yourself a mantra, like "May everything that lives be happy. May my thoughts, words, and actions contribute to that happiness." And to that first sentence, I have learned to add "including me." Buddhist teacher Jack Kornfield put it this way during an interview for *Lion's Roar*: "The circle of compassion is incomplete if one person is left out. Do you know who that person is? You. As Buddha said, you can search the entire tenfold universe and you will not find a single living being worth more to love than the one in your own home—you."

Metta Meditation

There are many variations of *metta* meditation, and I wholeheartedly recommend that you find a form that suits you and practice it. Just as no toolbox is complete without a hammer, no kitchen without a spoon, and no bath without a drain stopper, *metta* should be part of the basic practice of everyone who wants to live a lighter life. The lines below and on the next page are a good starting point. You can recite them out loud or mutter them softly to yourself. I often do that when I want to create distance between a (negative) primary and a secondary reaction or when I feel compassion and powerlessness.

First, look inward and say:

> *May I be happy.*
>
> *May I be healthy.*
>
> *May I be safe.*
>
> *May I live lightly.*

Now think of someone who makes you smile. That could be a loved one or perhaps a colleague—someone who has a positive presence in your life.

> *May you be happy.*
>
> *May you be healthy.*
>
> *May you be safe.*
>
> *May you live lightly.*

Then think of someone who leaves you neutral and indifferent because you don't really know her or him: the train conductor, someone who passes you on a bicycle, an acquaintance of an acquaintance.

May you be happy.

May you be healthy.

May you be safe.

May you live lightly.

Now think of someone who annoys you, who evokes something negative in you. Don't immediately think of your nemesis; practice first with someone who irritates you only a little bit. You can work up to practicing loving-kindness for the really tough people later.

May you be happy.

May you be healthy.

May you be safe.

May you live lightly.

Finally, complete the meditation with your intention for everything that lives: people, animals, nature.

May everything and everyone be happy.

May everything and everyone be healthy.

May everything and everyone be safe.

May everything and everyone live lightly.

WHAT
*are you
trying to
teach me?*

◇◇◇◇◇◇◇◇◇◇◇◇◇◇◇◇◇◇

YOUR
LOVELY
BODY
AND
BAD DAYS

◇◇◇◇◇◇◇◇◇◇◇◇◇◇◇◇◇◇

// The Soft Animal of Your Body

Why human touch is so important on hard days

I once had a massage therapist who told me that she regularly had clients who didn't have a specific problem. They didn't come to have a knot kneaded from their muscles or to prevent back issues; they had simply booked an appointment because of the touching itself, the pure sensation of skin on skin. It's known that, for babies and young children, being touched is essential for a secure bond and healthy emotional development. However, the fact that being touched is equally important for adults seems to have been somewhat brushed aside and forgotten in our culture. Placing your hand on someone's arm during a conversation, embracing a stranger—it isn't necessarily okay, because the way in which one enjoys being touched is highly personal.

But some form of physical contact, without any other intention than establishing a connection, is a pleasure you should allow yourself. In her poem "Wild Geese," Mary Oliver writes about "the soft animal of your body," an image I've always found beautiful and touching: your body as a soft animal, instinctive, primal, pure, full of life, no ego, no fuzz.

Just as a cat can surrender completely to a pet behind the ears and apes can spend hours grooming each other, the human body also relaxes when being touched. The feeling of a warm hand on your skin, someone combing your hair or giving you a warm hug is often more effective than any painkiller or other drug.

Touch consoles, comforts, connects, relaxes, energizes. It's primal. I can really experience skin hunger: I can jump in my car in the middle of the night and drive to another town just so I can cuddle up against the sleeping, breathing body of my boyfriend of the moment. It's a pure desire to occasionally just snuggle with someone without any further intentions. I'm still toying with the idea of a Tinder app for sleepers, for people who just want to nestle and nothing more.

Human touch scores well in scientific studies: It lowers blood pressure, causes the release of oxytocin (also known as the cuddle hormone), and lowers the level of cortisol, the stress hormone, in your blood. Touching boosts your immune system, enhances your sense of security, strengthens your confidence and self-love, and allows you to come home into your body. And on top of that, it is a balm for the soul.

Not everyone has easy access to human touch, though. There's a strong chance that on a bad day you'll have more physical contact with your phone than with a living person. Getting a massage is a really good idea on days when you're feeling meh, if only for your mental well-being. Or asking a friend for a hug. At our editorial office, I occasionally walk over to our office manager, Simone, who's always up for a firm hug. So nice and familiar. It doesn't happen often, but sometimes it simply *has* to happen.

Don't sidestep natural and casual physical affection, but let it be and relax about it. An arm, a leg—allow your body to experience intimacy, sex aside.

Give Yourself a
Little Shot of Oxytocin

◇◇◇◇◇◇◇◇◇◇◇◇◇◇

Not in the mood for other people on a bad day? Give
yourself a big hug, however cheesy that may sound. Cross
your arms and rub your upper arms. Your mind doesn't have
to agree. Allow yourself to feel ridiculous or pitiful; your body
will appreciate it in spite of you. Another method is to rub
yourself with a nice massage oil. Reassure the soft animal
of your body that everything is going to be all right again.

// A Tangerine on Your Chest

How your posture can improve your mood

A tangerine on your chest, a hundred-dollar bill between your buttocks, and an imaginary piece of string pulling you up by the crown of your head—that's how I was taught to stand up straight in ballet class. Try it sometime: It's a proud, powerful posture.

Often when people are having a lesser day, it shows a little in the way they carry themselves: shoulders drooping, back hunched, face glued to their screen, or staring down at the sidewalk. They walk sluggishly, swinging their arms like two soggy baguettes. Curling up like that can be nice and actually is quite soothing, when you're lying on the couch or in bed. The fetal position is super comfy, but standing erect can give you a little push in the right direction.

"Get your rear in gear!" I occasionally say to friends who have cloaked themselves in a heavy mantle of slackerdom. It's helpful to make your body do some of the work for you. Think about sayings like "chin up" or "stand tall" and you will immediately know what I mean.

Of course, you don't have to parade around like a happy camper if that is not at all how you feel. You can, however, make your body somewhat cooperate, if only to help you literally navigate your days with more lightness. Do this not for the outside world—although a positive body language can drastically alleviate your lesser days because you're giving off a different energy—but for yourself, for your inner world.

Using your body as a gently swaying, comfortable vehicle for the self enlightens your existence, more so than throwing your soul down the bumpy cobblestone path of life on a bike with wooden tires.

There is a lot of information available for those who have trouble finding a comfortable, natural body posture. But improving your posture doesn't necessarily mean an iron gym discipline or rigorous yoga training. Just being aware of the role you assign your body within the mind-body-soul trinity is a step in the right direction already.

Remember when we talked about the three-legged stool of mind, body, and soul? Each leg has to be of equal strength in order to perfectly balance life's weight. Your body is one of those supports enabling you to be well balanced. And life is simply lighter in a body that has fine-tuned the balance between effort and relaxation.

A light body allows free blood flow; your muscles can do what they need to do; your bones are all properly aligned—they have space, and nothing is forced; your breathing is more natural and free. A straight posture makes your clothes fit more elegantly and makes them feel more comfortable on your body. This has nothing to do with clothing size or beauty standards. Try to embody how you feel, or wish to feel, on the inside. Give your soul a nice home—soft, strong, and familiar.

Another valuable aspect of seeing your body as a "soft animal" is how the image emphasizes the importance of being gentle to it and taking good care of it. Often, we are too hard on our body. We force it into shapes, keep it going under the guise of "mind over matter," even after it starts to protest; we can even ignore its signals until a breaking point has been reached.

Take good care of your body, like you would care for a soft animal. Pat it. Feed it. Let it breathe. Cherish it. Brush it. Do not judge it. I know how hard this is; I too haven't always been nice to my body, not feeding it right and wishing it were different than it is. But by now I can sincerely say: Thank you, body. Thank you for your glorious imperfection, your quirkiness, and your love. I won't ever again force my body into submission.

On tough days, it helps to treat your body with dignity and respect. Mind and body belong together; they mirror each other. It isn't superficial to wash your hair and put on clean clothes. Neglecting your body because you are having a bad day can seem appealing. And it is perfectly fine to give your body some rest—to eat comfort food and to resist any kind of hassle. Don't let things get out of hand, though. Neglecting your body can become sloppiness and turn out to be just a quick fix that ultimately won't fix anything. Rarely does neglecting your body make your days actually lighter.

// Let's Talk about Sex for a Moment

This is the section my brothers might want to skip

I wish I had begun much, much earlier discussing and experiencing sex as freely as I have done during the past few years. Apparently, you need to be over thirty to do so. Or perhaps that delay happened to fit my personal development. Anyway, owning my sexual energy more freely has brought me many good things. I was neither prudish nor damaged in this department, but I did start to experience sex in a different way—and that has kept an equal pace with changes I've experienced in other aspects of my life.

Sex is a vulnerable topic. Although I have a healthy sense of self-worth, I of course do wonder sometimes how attractive I still am, sexually speaking. If you, like me, have given birth to two kids who were clearly above the national birthweight average, you didn't walk away unscathed. When I take off my clothes, you can read the barcode of my life on my body, and no personal trainer or cosmetic surgeon can magically return it to a blank slate. Do I wish I could trade in my kids for a porn-star body? No, of course not—I'm thankful for what this body can do and what it is giving me. Shapewear works magic, as does standing tall. Naked, however, is still just naked. Every body has a story and an ego that occasionally butts in.

Becoming free from my insecurity about this, even though it was "only" a subtle shift in energy, has been a good step in accepting things as they are. Sex is part of who we are. We are sexual beings, both men and women. Sex is good for your body, it's good for your energy, it's good for your soul.

Naturally, there are prerequisites: You should never do anything against your will, never hurt each other's feelings, and never jeopardize your health. Good sex doesn't sedate but instead awakens something. Sexual energy is an energy that can prove to be a game changer for some on bad days. Especially on those days, it can be so wonderful to love someone, to release energy, to give up control for a bit, and to be very close to yourself and your desires.

And if you don't have a lover, be your own. Sexual energy is life energy, it's creative energy, it's tantric energy, and it's a part of our essence. Don't deny yourself that, because the flame, however small, is burning inside each of us. Sex causes that spark in your underbelly that ignites something positive.

If you are insecure or become all giggly when sex is involved, it's time to explore why that is. Looking at myself, the way to freedom also coincided with letting go of the expectations others had of me. Above all, sex is not about perfection. In the heat of the moment, it really doesn't matter how flattering your pose is or whether your mascara is running. On the contrary, sex is about accepting imperfection: the ability to be naked, vulnerable, and primal in the company of yourself and someone else. In that sense, sex is a spiritual exercise.

Of course, feeling sexy on lesser days is a complicated matter. I'm not always in the mood for physical fuss, let alone for parting with my comfy socks and fluffy pink cardigan. But there are also plenty of situations when I thank my lover of the moment for the opportunity to let that sexual energy flow. The endorphins you produce during a bedroom romp work as a natural pain reliever and tranquilizer. Basically, sex is a great way to relax while also having some fun, if you're in the mood for it. I like saying it: Explore! Make your pleasure a priority.

// Sleep Is Sacred

Zen starts with z's

If the shortcuts in this handbook were to be ranked, sleep would, without a doubt, end up in the top ten. The relationship between bad days and bad sleep is so direct, so evident, and so essential that sleep assumes a prominent spot among the shortcuts to a lighter life. Whenever I'm struggling—when I'm moody, listless, or melancholic—one of the first things I do is trace my recent sleeping patterns. And sure enough, you can bet that my previous night's routine was, at least, irregular.

For years, I was able to sleep effortlessly and deeply, so it took me quite a while before I saw the link between my inner peace and my sleep cycle. Ten years ago, I was able to fall asleep anytime and anywhere: on the floor of an airport terminal, in noisy hostels, on collapsed couches— no problem. But those days are over. Now I know what sleeplessness is, as well as sleep deprivation, and how that affects how I'm feeling. That knowledge sometimes prevents me from endlessly ruminating on what is making me feel so meh. Now I know: I need to get a couple of good nights' sleep. The way you sleep is the way you live.

Just get a couple of good nights' sleep—I know, I know . . . easier said than done. Especially when your mind or body are super wired, it can be difficult to let go and surrender yourself to sleep. Sometimes sleep is an unwanted interruption of a busy life; better to first get that quick glass of wine, do some channel surfing, and maybe answer some e-mails instead of wasting precious time sleeping.

Eat, breathe, sleep: Those are the three sacred and essential elements of your Mental Discomfort First Aid kit. If a friend calls me in panic, sorrow, or other trouble, I listen well and then give them more or less the only sound advice I can offer: Make sure you keep eating, breathe as relaxed and deep as you can, and sleep. These are the basic necessities of life on good days, and especially on bad ones.

How much sleep you need depends on your personal circumstances, but broadly speaking you can divide your days into three eight-hour blocks: eight hours of work and activity, eight hours of relaxation and nourishment, eight hours of rest. Sleep is part of that daily cycle, generally between sunset and sunrise. It's a rhythm to which we all move: up and down, ebb and flow, day and night, activity and rest.

Science has often linked sleep to our health, both mental and physical. It has everything to do with how your brain works and with your body's self-healing ability. In order to be resilient, you need to give your body the opportunity to replenish itself, uninterrupted, for hours at a time.

Did you know that the soul also goes to sleep at night? In Islam and certain Jewish traditions, as well as some other spiritual circles, there's a saying that during the night, the soul returns to the source. Regardless of whether you call this source the creator or the light or something else, you can imagine the following: The soul replenishes itself at night in order to return to the body recharged the next morning.

That is why, in many religions, the morning prayer is a thanksgiving prayer, an expression of gratitude for the returned soul and the new day. It's a beautiful idea, isn't it, the thought of being plugged in to a mystic charger each night? The notion that you can receive epiphanies at night is also interesting. "Sleeping on something" isn't just an excuse for postponing a decision; it really is a good idea. At night, your subconscious mind keeps going, which is why you can sometimes wake up with a decision or a solution, just like that. Your own internal system installs updates at night, just like your computer. On bad days, good sleep hygiene is an extra form of self-care.

Devote the same attention to the room where you sleep as to your workspace and the area where you relax. The idea that "nobody's going to see it anyway" is only partly true: A pleasant and serene bedroom gives you the space to truly relax and is a sanctuary on lesser days.

Tend to Your Bed

◇◇◇◇◇◇◇◇◇◇◇◇◇◇

Invest in a quality mattress and nice bed linens. Climbing into a hotel bed every night—that's how comfortable your sheets and covers should be.

Make your bed in the morning, so that in the evening you find a bed that's inviting to slide into—a bed that exudes care, as if someone (you) is taking good care of you.

Make sure your bedroom is cool and well-ventilated. Nothing is more depressing than wallowing in your own stale sleepiness.

Leave your electronic devices in another room. It really makes a difference.

In general, having screens in the bedroom is a bad idea, because of both the electromagnetic radiation and the distraction. Bookcases or other types of open closets don't belong in the bedroom either; they are "active" elements, whereas your bedroom should have a more subdued energy.

Feng shui specialist Nina Elshof once told me an interesting fact: For our bedroom, we tend to choose the largest room in the house, and we make the smaller ones the home office or children's rooms. It's better to do the opposite: Large rooms, where you are surrounded by open space and where energy can flow freely, make better workspaces. Smaller rooms are more like cocoons with a single, clear function: resting.

If your daily rhythm allows, synchronize your sleep schedule with the daylight cycle.

Thirty minutes before going to bed, reduce all triggers. Dim the light, lower the volume . . .

Make sure that your room is sufficiently dark. I also wear a sleeping mask, which prevents me from opening my eyes during phases of light slumber.

Whenever my mind is busy, I listen to relaxing music. It gives me a point of fixation. My favorite sleep soundtracks are those based on so-called delta waves, low-frequency sounds that somehow have a calming effect on your brain and are associated with a state of deep sleep. Meditation apps are generally a good place for finding soundtracks that can help you fall asleep.

// Why It's Better to Just Get Up

The morning is friendlier than you think

I know: It's no fun waking up on bad days. The hours stretch out before you like a vast ice-skating rink. Another day, another gray. Another twelve hours to survive before you can pull the covers over your head and disappear back into a deep sleep. And I'll admit right away that I'm no morning person. I'm a world champion in snoozing, rolling over, and procrastinating. For years, I've sabotaged my days and undermined my mood this way, and only now that I've established (some sort of) a morning routine am I able to look back and think: What a waste of energy.

I thought that staying in bed a little longer meant I was treating myself to some extra rest. But the opposite was true: After lingering in the no-man's-land between sleeping and waking, I began those days messy and hasty. It takes more energy than it delivers to stay in bed just those few extra moments each morning.

That isn't to say that I had some sort of evangelical "and then I saw the light!" moment, because in truth I more or less stumbled upon this insight. And I had kids. During their first years, I was forced to get up when they called me. Afterward, when that was no longer the case, I actually lost the ability to enjoy sleeping in. Correction: At first, I called this "lost the ability to do it"; now I prefer "learned how to not do it."

Early-morning light is a balm for the soul. The morning carries the promise of "another day, another chance," and if you manage to tap into that, your day will take on a whole different kind of energy.

There are books suggesting that you start your day around 5:00 or 5:30 a.m. I find that a little too early myself, but I applaud people who can actually pull it off. There is a milder version that might suit you. A good starting point is to get up an hour earlier than you want to. If that feels daunting, start half an hour earlier. Or perhaps start with fifteen minutes.

What you want to do with that extra time is to keep your mind in check. Because as soon as you wake up, your brain will kick into gear: What are my tasks for today, who am I going to meet, and what do I think and expect? Building in a morning routine will save your monkey mind a lot of energy, enabling you to start the day slowly.

What your ideal morning routine might look like depends on quite a few external factors: how many people you share your mornings with, whether or not you have a job that requires you to show up at a certain time, whether or not you have to prepare lunch, whether or not you insist on curling your hair and "putting your face on." Why don't you start by charting your absolute must-dos, and think about how you can breathe some air into those? And there definitely are a few general tips for those moments. The ideal morning routine for your soul is not about winning time and optimizing. It's about being present and about managing energy. Perhaps try a few of these suggestions:

Stand in front of an open window. And—who cares if the neighbors are watching—seamlessly stretch out your arms, channeling Kate Winslet on the deck of the *Titanic*, and take a deep breath. This one deep breath of fresh morning air connects you with the whole waking world.

Do some stretching. Your body will thank you.

Come up with a resolution and say it out loud. This will set the tone for the day. It doesn't immediately have to be some grand statement, let alone anything poetic. Perhaps something along the lines of "Today I'll take some time for myself" or just a single word. Drawing a motivational card can also help. Those are often heartwarming, well thought-out, and inspiring. If you're in a bad mood, however, "Make it through the day" will suffice.

Eat something you enjoy eating, and drink something you enjoy drinking—things you *really* enjoy eating and drinking. Fast and convenient can go hand in hand, along with nutritious and good. Quality coffee, freshly made tea. Delicious granola, fresh fruits. The subtle difference between fueling up and feeding yourself can color your day.

Download your thoughts: Quickly write down what's important.

Try to insert a moment of silence, if only for five minutes, in which you sit down and do *nothing*. I swear by meditating in the morning, however briefly.

Leave your phone and other screens alone for as long as possible. This will help you stick to initiating instead of reacting. Doing this tends to save a lot of energy in the morning. Make up your own mind about what you plan to do before your devices take charge.

Get dressed with care, and consider what you'll be needing that day to feel comfortable. I can get really annoyed when I'm forced to just slip on whatever—not because of what other people might say but because my clothes affect my energy.

   I prefer soft fabrics and calm colors whenever I need to concentrate, and I want flouncy dresses when I have something to celebrate. On days when I just pull something from the closet, I feel messier and less focused. And if I can avoid having a bad day by putting on a top without stains and tights that don't sag, that's a small price to pay. Balance the outside with the inside.

// Keep Breathing

Seems obvious, but read this tip anyway

Please don't forget to keep breathing. You might feel cheated when reading a suggestion like this. I mean, it doesn't require much thought: Breathing is something we do automatically, right? In, out, in, out, all day, every day, and as long as you continue doing it, you'll stay alive. Taking a breath is the first thing we do when we're born and the last thing we do before we move on. It really is one of our most basic activities: breathing in, breathing out.

Yet there is breathing, and then there is *breathing.* Taking a breath is more than simply making sure your organs are supplied with oxygen.

As teacher and yogi Max Strom said so beautifully and aptly: "The lungs are the engines of our emotional communication. Through our breath we express how we feel: rushed, excited, tired, or upset."

What's more, your lungs provide a lot more potential than you probably are using right now. Did you know that most people are using not even half of their maximum lung capacity? In general, we take fleeting, shallow breaths and fill our lungs to only one-third of their capacity. Under stress, we tend to breathe even more shallowly, as if we are in a state of alert. Our lungs may contain air, but most of the time, making optimal use of fresh air isn't something we do automatically. If we aren't paying attention to our breath, our lungs become more like a partly deflated flamingo floating around at a pool party. Not very festive.

Have you ever experienced someone who was mildly hysterical? Someone who had completely lost it because of panic, anger, or shock? You may feel an urge to, as they do in the movies, dramatically slap such a person across their face with the flat of your hand. That impulse doesn't necessarily stem from a theatrical or aggressive personality but is, in fact, very natural: the startling effect of such a blow will leave the other person gasping for air. And that gasp of air is exactly what is needed for them to snap out of the hysteria. The good news is that you may save yourself from having a red mark on your face by simply being more mindful of the way you breathe when you're overwhelmed or anxious.

Breathing is about—and, yes, here we go again—balance. It shifts you away from your head and to your body, from the rush to the calmness.

EVELINE HELMINK

Inhale, exhale. That's how simple it can be to return to the present moment and shake off a lesser day. A calm breath does so many good things for you: Your body can draw in more oxygen to do what it needs to do, your stress level goes down, tension melts into relaxation.

If you find it hard to use your breathing to achieve calmness and control, there are many courses and workshops that can teach you proper technique—and they are totally worth it. But a simple breathing exercise can be done anywhere, including in the line at the supermarket, in front of a bar, and hidden inside your one-night-stand's bathroom.

The first step: Breathe in through your nose. It's made for the job: The nasal hairs filter out particulate matter, and your nose detects smells, which makes you more aware of your environment and anchors you in the present moment. Of our five senses, we especially like to rely on our sight, hearing, taste, and touch, but smell is an equally important compass.

Step two is to, little by little, let your breathing go deeper, in a natural tempo. Breathing deeply will make not only your chest swell, because of your air-filled lungs, but also your midriff, flanks, and belly.

Step three: When exhaling, let the air escape slowly, unforced. If you turn this simple deep-breathing technique into a routine, you'll notice that it really is a universal tool, one that deserves to be advertised alongside infomercials for magic wonder sponges and miracle veggie slicers.

A calm breath makes you less easily irritated, less "on," less restless or nervous. Simply put, you're more relaxed, more focused and productive, and more pleasant company for others and yourself.

Davidji, an American meditation teacher, often shares his sixteen-second meditation as an antidote to the "coulda, woulda, shoulda" rumination cycle, which could very well be the mantra of many a bad day. The trick is to take short breaks between inhaling and exhaling, a technique also extolled by other breathing specialists. Those are tiny moments of surrender. The breathing exercise goes like this: Inhale for four seconds and hold that breath for four seconds. Exhale for four seconds and hold that breath for another four seconds. Imagine a lemniscate, also known as the infinity symbol. Outside going inward, inside going outward. It's simple and effective. Just give it a try.

// Take a Hot Shower

Solace, right from your own faucet

One of the most underestimated home remedies for mitigating a bad day is the shower. You may think that you need at least a full spa day to relax, but however nice it can be to dream of steam cabins and baths filled with rose petals, every household has a shower, and every shower is suitable for soothing the pains of hard days.

Ask a screenwriter to situate a mental breakdown inside a home, and you can be sure that the bathroom will end on the short list of likely locations. You can already imagine the scene: the actor hunched on the floor, hugging his knees, in solitude. Sinking down on the bathroom floor is a common practice on bad days—the door can be locked, there's very little else to do there, and the tiles are cool. It is precisely there, where you're broken, that something will germinate.

And since you're in the bathroom anyway, the shower is within (crawling) reach. Sure, the bathtub has a better reputation. We associate it with wellness, relaxation, soaking, and taking time. I've spent hours and hours in the bathtub while contemplating life's big questions. Being enveloped in warm water can be soothing. But don't disregard the shower. To be honest, I'd even argue that on really bad days the shower is the better choice. It's the running water. Whatever you rinse off immediately disappears through the drain. After a hot shower, I always instantly feel less gray, less dusty, less meh.

The sound of running water alone is the most calming and natural sound there is. It's white noise, a sound that incorporates every conceivable pitch. It calms your brain, which will no longer need to differentiate between various sensory stimuli. There's a reason New Age stores sell soundtracks of tropical rainstorms, and a shower has more or less the same effect, with the advantage that it's live.

Another benefit of taking a shower: It will bring you lucid insights. Because you are just standing there, water trickling down your skin, your conscious and subconscious mind will start flowing. Various scientific research substantiates this: It appears that warm water stimulates the release of dopamine, while also helping your body to relax; as a result, your physical body demands less attention.

This leads us to the third benefit of taking a shower: It warms your body. You'll find that many spiritual books advocate taking cold showers, and they do have their benefits. But let's not forget what warm water can do for you. The warmth stimulates blood circulation, and when the idea of any real exercise feels like too much, anything that can promote better oxygen distribution is very welcome. The hot water will relax your muscles and joints, and your pores will open up, allowing you to rinse off the dirt from your body and sweat out anything you don't need. Taking a shower is a natural tranquilizer for the mind, the body, and the soul. Taking a shower is a wonderful ritual.

In spiritual practice, water is an essential element, widely regarded as the conduit of energy. Running water restores balance to anything that is out of whack; it calms and purifies. Water symbolizes the emotional life and feelings and is the basis for all life. And it comes from your own faucet.

The next time you take a shower, try this: Visualize washing off all your worries and seeing them disappear down the drain. Imagine all the negative energy that was hanging around you being scrubbed away. Running water is movement, and movement is change, and change offers possibilities.

// Crying Is a Form of Detoxing

I'm a crybaby, but it's self-care

And you know what I really crave on a bad day? A serious, dramatic crying fit. It is *such* a release! Not everyone understands tears. In fact, most people find tears difficult and prefer not to see them. At the sight of tears, people are quick to console, comfort, contextualize, brush off, or look away. Crying is associated with a loss of control; it is considered weak, childish, overly dramatic, or inappropriate. And that makes extensive crying in company, especially at unexpected moments, slightly uncomfortable and a tad embarrassing: "I'm sorry I'm crying, but . . ." Sound familiar? I think most of us can recognize that moment of bursting into tears and watching the people around you become dismayed and anxious.

I don't mean to sound unkind, but men in particular can be totally clueless when it comes to tears; they have no idea how to react. On the one hand, there's a biological explanation for this: Men have fewer of the hormones associated with tears. And on the other, it's culturally determined: Boys shouldn't cry. *Generally*, men who cry are seen as weak. I like to emphasize the word "generally" because I know quite a few men who do show their emotions. In any case, crying isn't something we as a society know how to deal with elegantly.

I often ask myself: Why can't we just take crying for what it is? Can't we just all agree that we don't necessarily need to stop someone from crying with soothing words, hastily fetched glasses of water, and awkward hugs? I would like to make a case for learning how to deal with crying less awkwardly. Just sit down next to someone, wrap an arm around them, and let the tears flow, with deep confidence that they will slow down on their own.

We humans aren't made to control our emotions. Tears have a purpose. They show that you need help or support. When you are able to allow and display your vulnerability, you offer the people around you the opportunity to really see you.

In that sense, hiding your tears reinforces the issue of loneliness: *Doesn't anybody see how I'm feeling?* As a matter of fact, no, they don't. If you're hiding your feelings, people can't always intuit them from looking at you. When you don't show your emotions—and that doesn't necessarily mean just no crying, of course—and when you repress what you're feeling, your emotions turn inward. When you don't cry or find another way to somehow convey your emotions, they morph into stress, depression, or a great many lesser days.

But aside from what others think or do about crying, once in a while shedding tears can actually be a great solo activity. You can see tears as words or feelings that cannot be articulated: energy from your heart and your body finding its way out. It's a pure, natural, and powerful way to let go.

There's no consensus in the scientific community about the purpose of emotional tears, but one hypothesis is that tears help release stress hormones and that tears contain a chemical that functions as a natural painkiller. Although scientists may not know exactly how this works, I find it a wonderful idea—that our body is a subtle instrument for the soul that helps us express what our logical mind can't translate into language. Your own body consoling you, the rhythm of a crying fit, the way your body shakes—it's like the cadence of a mother consoling a baby; it's how you were rocked when you were still inside your mother's womb. While you're crying, you comfort yourself. It's delightful how our body and soul can work together so self-sufficiently.

I tear up easily. I cry out of an excess of emotion, out of sadness, frustration, rage, gratitude, compassion, or happiness. I'm not afraid of tears, I don't try to avoid them, and I'm rarely embarrassed by them either.

Most of my memories of sobbing are precious. Not because they were so much fun. At the least, they were not the kind of memories you wish were documented in photographs because you would like to revisit them. It's a different kind of precious. These were intimate moments during which things were marked or transformed, because they were moments of profound processing and, sporadically, of personal growth.

I remember the time I was heartbroken and crashed at my friends' place. How, in the middle of the night, I woke up in tears on a mattress on the floor of their study. I remember how I walked over to their bedroom, and how he didn't seem to find that strange, and how she joined me downstairs and sat with me on the couch in a dark living room, wrapping the two of us in a blanket and rocking me until the tears ran out. No questions asked, no judgment.

I remember after an intense workout, tears were running down my cheeks at the gym. It wasn't just the tension in my muscles from the physical workout that was flowing from my body, but also the emotional marathon that I was running in my personal life. I cry during school performances and charity walks and children's choirs, because the innocence of those cheerfully marching children and their confidence that life is beautiful, good, and fun is so pure.

I remember the existential tears I shed at the ER when I arrived to learn that my eldest son, six at the time, had been hit by a motorbike: *my* child. I remember the hot tears of anger and outrage. All the tears I ever cried have drawn my attention to or reminded me of something. In the same way drops of water are like a magnifying glass, tears are too. They show us what is precious, true, and pure.

There's a Jewish saying that what soap is to the body, tears are to the soul. Sometimes the tears won't come. There were times when I knew it had to happen, that a good cry would be a relief, moments when I really went for it, yet without a single tear welling up in my eyes. Not one. All the while there was a lingering feeling inside that something was trying to find its way out. Sound familiar?

When you need to jump-start a good cry, look for a pleasant spot where you can physically relax—one that is warm, safe. Put on some melodramatic music. Don't breathe to escape the sadness, but instead breathe toward it. Dive deeper and deeper into the essence of a face, a situation, or a feeling.

When the tears *do* appear, keep breathing calmly. Allow your body to do what it needs to do. Perhaps one large tear is all you can muster that day, or perhaps you will achieve an ugly cry—deep sobs and red eyes and all; however it swells, ride out the wave till the end, until you wash up on dry land. Crying fits are never endless, although in the moment one may feel that way. After a time, they ebb away. Crying is an energy shift, like a spiral taking you ever deeper and inward, to the essence, to the core. Follow your tears.

// **Once Around the Block**

Walking is the rhythm of the soul

I'm not really the outdoorsy type. I don't own hiking boots or high-tech rain gear or step-counting waistbands. I find being indoors comfortable and warm. Still, I discovered how soul-soothing walking can be on a bad day. Just going from A to B on foot. From my house to the supermarket. Around the block. Or—let's live a little—a stroll in the park.

Walking is the rhythm of the soul, I once heard someone say. It's one of the oldest, most natural, simple, and accessible ways to move from one place to another. Transporting ourselves like that is part of who we are. Our body enjoys the cadence, the steady pace. There's a reason most pilgrims go on foot; the activity of walking is like praying.

Of course, there are also physical health benefits to walking: Your pulse will get into a pleasant rhythm, your lungs will fill up with nice fresh air, and your blood circulation will definitely be better than after five hours of binge-watching Netflix. Numerous health benefits are attributed to hiking. But being outside also literally means you have more space. There's nothing between you and the sky. It's very easy to see walking as a metaphor for life itself: finding your way, moving forward, turning corners . . .

It took quite some time before I heeded the wisdom to go for a walk on a bad day. Then one day, out of pure restlessness, I changed my comfy socks for sneakers, put on my headphones, and began to cover some serious distances on foot. Today it's one of my go-to routines when I'm experiencing a lesser day. Walking organizes my thoughts; it has a calming effect on my body, and it soothes my heart. Often a sudden idea or understanding pops into my head while I'm putting one foot in front of the other. There's nothing to do besides walk; no matter what direction you're heading in, you have to walk. It's an activity that creates space for new thoughts.

The gospel that walking benefits the soul has been proclaimed by spiritual teachers, coaches, and even psychologists for centuries. Thich Nhat Hahn, a Buddhist monk, has written several books on the topic; the documentary about his life is aptly titled *Walk with Me*. He says: "The true miracle is not walking on water or walking in air, but simply walking on this earth." When you're attentive to the everyday things, with each step you take you'll discover just how miraculous everything is. How miraculously simple.

At times, to walk is nothing more than shaking out that negative energy. In *Happinez* magazine, travel journalist and philosopher Anne Wesseling shared an anecdote about the Inuit: When they're really angry, they furiously leave their home on foot and holding a stick. They continue to walk, walk, walk, cutting across the landscape in a straight line until they feel their anger subsiding. On the spot where they are able to let go of their anger, they plant the stick in the snow, as a witness to the extent of their outrage. Then they walk back home. Perhaps we could start carrying pieces of chalk in our pockets to do the same?

If hiking suits you, you can turn it into a lifestyle. Hiking is a total scene; there are countless books, clubs, trails, and coaches. There's no reason to immediately become all serious, or mindful, and meditative about it, though. Don't force overly ambitious or lofty goals on yourself if you don't feel like it. No "I will walk at least seven miles" or "When I return, I'll have come up with a solution." Don't sweat it. Just pull your hoodie over your head, kick yourself into gear, and take a few steps.

Walking versus Running

◇◇◇◇◇◇◇◇◇◇◇◇◇◇◇

Running is a tried and tested means to get out of a negative mindset, but hiking is a little less arduous on your body. Especially when you're full of adrenaline, it is a good idea to not "whip up" your body even more, but to calm it instead. When you are nervous or under a lot of stress, you don't want to end up with even higher energy. Moreover, all you need for a stroll around the block are some shoes and perhaps a coat; you can go for a walk on a whim, no matter where you are.

FOOD
FOR
THOUGHT

// Giving Up *Is* an Option

You don't have to continue to muddle through

It can feel like an incredibly painful split, the realization that you've thrown in the towel while everyone, including yourself, is shouting, "Don't give up!" I, on the other hand, am a fan of giving up, at least now and again. There's nothing wrong with recognizing that the path you had in mind apparently isn't your destiny. That it's costing you more than it's giving you. So you note that, in spite of all your good intentions and serious efforts, the thing you wanted appears or remains unattainable.

Giving up can be a powerful decision. When you're able to be honest with yourself, you can let go of your rigidity, detach yourself from all those "shoulds." Giving up isn't defeat. You are liberating yourself from expectations and judgments. It can be such a relief! But, but . . . can you give up and still make progress? Of course you can! Giving up doesn't mean you have to let go of your goal. Rather, it may be time to reassess that goal, to explore other avenues, to check detours.

It may be time for a time-out.

What a waste, you might be thinking. *A waste of all that time I put in, the energy I put out, the money and effort I've already invested. A waste of a dream.* To some extent, I blame the current zeitgeist and all the ideas about designing your own life and directing your own success. That mindset has become so dominant that, deep down, we believe we deserve what we want, while reality is far more erratic and illusive.

More often than not, perseverance is driven by ego. Maybe you know the heartbreaking stories of mountaineers who wanted to attain the top of Mount Everest at all costs. Using their final reservoir of strength, they reached the summit. They made it—or should that be "achieved" it? The climber is now officially a hero, a true go-getter. But most mountaineers who die don't expire on the ascent or at the top; they die on the way down. They've pocketed the desired result, but all their strength has been depleted, all their oxygen used up. On that merciless and cruel mountain, it's often not a fatal event or inclement weather that causes climbers to collapse, but rather extreme exhaustion, something they didn't anticipate after reaching their goal.

Perseverance for its own sake is highly valued in our culture. Just consider the many "inspirational" quotes reminding us of this fact: "Winners never quit, quitters never win!" or "Pain is acceptable, quitting is not!" or "Fall down seven times, get up eight!" or "No pain, no gain!" All nonsense.

Of course, perseverance is important. Sometimes you have to push yourself beyond what you think you're capable of. That's how growth happens: try, and try, and try again. The key is recognizing when you've hit a wall. At what point are you buzzing against a windowpane over and over again like a fly, never even noticing the glass? Oh, I know very well how that feels. When it comes to love, I've had to learn that lesson countless times, and the same goes for other aspects of my life.

Giving up requires self-examination and being able to recognize (and accept) what is. You and *only* you can know whether the energy you're putting toward your goal is balanced with the energy you expect to receive when you reach it. Discovering that your energy is stagnating and that you've reached a stalemate can be painful and raw. Saying goodbye to a dream or goal is a moment of grief. Allow yourself to be angry or disappointed. By the time the fog clears, all that will be left is space. Space for something new, something better.

When Should I
Call It Quits?

◇◇◇◇◇◇◇◇◇◇◇◇◇◇◇

When you suspect you may be persevering for the sake of achievement
or habit or ego, try asking yourself these questions. Depending on your
answers, it may be time for a detour:

- *Is this something I want to achieve or something I feel I should achieve?*
- *Does my motivation for this goal come from the outside or from within?*
- *Who would be happiest if I reached this goal?*
- *Who would be the most disappointed if I didn't?*
- *How would it feel if I let go of this?*
- *What would take its place?*

// Advanced Complaining
Bitching, moaning, and whining

Life will always find ways to be unkind to you. When you think about it, there really isn't a way to escape the tormenting that's part of this temporary earthly existence. You will get wrinkles, you'll be disappointed, you'll lose what is dear to you. Even if you start a utopian commune with only like-minded people on a remote mountaintop, you still won't be spared the headwinds of adversity. Things happen, both good *and* bad things. And complaining about it is pretty futile; fundamentally, it doesn't make much of a difference. Whining is not the most attractive look, and when you don't give it some structure, it isn't particularly constructive either.

Having said that, a nice, comprehensive jeremiad does have its pluses, if only because it's exhausting to always be the controlled, well-balanced, and polite version of yourself. Once in a while, you need to vent. Oh, what a relief it can be to blow off steam! Sometimes everything that is bothering, annoying, grieving, hurting, touching, and irritating you needs to be discharged. Once in a while, it can feel *so* nice to open the windows to let out all those stuffy grievances and free up space for fresh, clean air.

Complaining doesn't need to be pointless if you handle it wisely, employing it as a release of everything that's irrational, melodramatic, unfounded, primal, unreasonable, and nonsensical. I compare it to weeding the garden of your mind: Weeds keep growing, whether you like it or not, and if you don't do regular upkeep, they can overgrow your garden and obstruct the light for all the plants you actually want to grow there.

That nagging, whiny voice just wants to be heard once in a while. Sometimes it's embarrassing to listen to and sometimes pretty funny; sometimes it can fill you with compassion, and in the best case, you'll listen to yourself and think: Oh, so that's what's bothering me. Perhaps you hear your inner child, who has learned how to behave but now wants to claim a moment for unreasonable defiance. Maybe it's your caring self, who thinks you could've taken better care of yourself. In the residue of your protest you might find a pure insight.

Turn that junk drawer in your head upside down and survey what's inside: Which thought is worth keeping, which should be somewhere else, and which can be discarded? I often find it's satisfying to combine this mental spring cleaning with physical exercise: Scratch on a sheet of paper, squeeze a pillow, tear pieces of cardboard, run a mile.

Advanced Complaining in Practice

◇◇◇◇◇◇◇◇◇◇◇◇◇◇◇◇◇

Venting to someone may be nice, but consider the time and place. Birthday parties, working colleagues, a complete stranger on a train: perhaps not the right moment, perhaps not the right audience.

Direct your diatribes back to the facts and to reality. It's easy to land in a ditch when putting the pedal to the metal. Moderate, shift gears, and hit the brakes in time.

Don't make complaining an unconscious habit or a go-to strategy to distract attention from yourself. Vent your gripes, but be fully mindful of what you say and how you say it. Turn your dissatisfaction into an exercise, not an attitude.

Remember: Voicing your grievances should give you air, not add *more* to the weight you're carrying. The energy should be released, not absorbed.

Look for a partner in crime. For years, I worked with someone I could call on when I occasionally wanted to blow off steam, without consequences or any particular outcome. Afterward, I would return to the issues of the day relieved and with more perspective. All she'd do was shrug her shoulders and tell me I was right, no matter what. Most of the time, that was all I needed.

Smile at yourself and smile about your unreasonableness. Sometimes complaining is just like stand-up comedy. Try listening with that perspective: If you don't identify with what you're going on about, it can be hilariously unreasonable. Remember: You are not your thoughts.

Once you're done venting, ask yourself the final question: So, now what? Is there something you need to announce? Do you need to examine something? Maybe the answer is "nothing," and that's fine too. Put an end to it. Be done with it. Let go.

// The Beginner's Mind

The freedom of not knowing

The famously charming and adventurous Pippi Longstocking once declared, "I have never tried that before, so I think I should definitely be able to do that!" While somewhat foolhardy, this is also a wise sentiment. Zen Buddhism would call this "the beginner's mind" or *shoshin*. The best definition has probably been given by Zen master Shunryu Suzuki (1904–1971): "If your mind is empty, it is always ready for anything; it is open to everything. In the beginner's mind there are many possibilities; in the expert's mind there are few."

The beginner's mind is an attitude of openness, of eagerness. It's a combination of being present in the middle of the situation, involved and with full attention, while simultaneously floating a little above it, detached and unbiased. It's like the mind of a child: attentive and intense, as if everything is happening for the first time. A beginner's mind can help you slow down and observe what is happening without judgment or preconceived ideas. It is a gratifying attitude that brings a feeling of calmness and control.

Ever since I was introduced to this notion and began to apply it to my life, I've been experiencing more space, more freedom. I'm no longer living a life of exclamation points, but rather one of question marks: a life that is dynamic, open, and fully aimed at possibilities. Consider these words Rainer Maria Rilke wrote in a letter to an aspiring poet: "Be patient toward all that is unsolved in your heart and try to love the questions themselves, like locked rooms and like books that are now written in a very foreign tongue. Do not now seek the answers, which cannot be given you because you would not be able to live them. And the point is, to live everything. Live the questions now. Perhaps you will then gradually, without noticing it, live along some distant day into the answer."

When you think you know something for certain, when you are fully convinced, you pretty much always sacrifice an amount of objectivity and perspective. When looking at a problem objectively, with a beginner's mind, you will leave out a lot of interpretation, assumptions, and opinions.

What use is it to learn or to gain experiences and insights if you are forced to put them aside anyway? I asked this question of Zen master

Bernie Glassman (1939–2018), whom I was fortunate enough to interview. He answered that the more knowledge you gather, the better, that you could see knowledge as something you fill up a large backpack with. Learn as many languages as you can, go for any diploma you can obtain, and read every book that interests you. The problem begins once you get *attached* to what you know, if you approach life armed with only one particular piece of knowledge. Only when you're open and present can you reach into your backpack for knowledge that can help you to act lovingly.

And then it helps if your backpack is fully packed. Knowledge is beautiful and valuable, but knowing a lot doesn't automatically mean you possess the *right* knowledge. With an open attitude, you can acquire knowledge without being dominated by it. When you understand what a situation calls for, it will automatically become clear to you what is needed. Not knowing isn't the end; it's a wonderful beginning.

In practice, having a beginner's mind means taking a step back. And that isn't always easy. After all, our brains are filled with countless well-trodden paths and ingrained ideas, all aimed at helping us reach conclusions or solutions at lightning speed. It's good that we don't apply our beginner's mind to everything we do; this saves us from considering twenty-seven ways to tie our shoelaces, cook spaghetti, or cross an intersection. It's comforting to know *the one way* to do that. This "knowing," however, tends to dominate our mind. We may think we have a solution for everything. And that's where the frustrating, cosmic game of cat-and-mouse begins: We think we have an answer to everything, and then we experience something we can't comprehend or place, and we are thrown off balance.

Your certainties are the bars that keep you locked in your own box, while there's a whole wide world outside. The beginner's mind helps you stay open to what is, without immediately interpreting or rejecting it. It's a mindset that requires a little practice, but nevertheless one that leads to a lighter life.

// On Grief

Saying goodbye is real, and it f*king hurts

"It happens to everyone. But you feel it alone" is the most striking remark on grief I've ever read. It's a quote from Helen McDonald's *H Is for Hawk*, a book she wrote when she had to say goodbye to her father. Grief is a common thread in human life. Even though we associate it with death, the irreversible goodbye, grief is actually part of quotidian affairs, like dropping a beautiful vase or the cancellation of the weekly lunches you'd been having with your best friend because she moved to the other side of the country. It's the essence of our existence: We arrive and we leave; things come, things go. Yet we passionately resist that impermanence.

The passing of things remains a profound, painful, heartbreaking lesson. Those who take the spiritual path will acquire insights in order to detach themselves from this suffering, but I suspect that, for most of us earthly souls, grieving will remain a lifelong struggle. Grief is part of us.

Farewell and loss: My very worst days are characterized by these sentiments. I've felt grief in my body, in my soul, and it's paralyzing. Many nights on end, I lay awake, haunted by the sensation that the Velcro connecting me and someone I loved was slowly tearing loose: my mother, to whom, due to her dementia, I was forced to say goodbye, little by little, or a great love who turned out to be a passerby. Grief leaves little room for other things; even eating or sleeping are pushed to the background. It's an invisible bell jar that is placed over you and that keeps everything and everyone at a distance, while life outside continues as usual. "Numb" is the word we use to describe this feeling.

Grief is one of the most difficult emotions for me to control. I've always found it hard to deal with transience. Things that pass, imperfection, and frayed edges form the heart of my practice, and not without reason; for me, that's where the biggest lessons in life are to be found, and that's what attracts my interest time and time again. Perhaps it's in part because grief was the first truly overwhelming emotion that crossed my path; I lost my best friend at age twelve. Over the past twenty-five years, I've often thought that I had adequately healed from that experience, that it "hadn't left a mark." To a certain extent, that is the case: I'm still here, standing strong. Even so, my heart has a scar. I had just entered middle school and hadn't experienced anything yet, and at the same time, I'd experienced everything. Grieving as a child is extra complicated. Till this day my heart burns when I think about that period.

Grief is a daily phenomenon. With each day, we die a little. Life's path is riddled with holes from things falling away. Grief is the answer to the loss we experience, and that sense of mourning starts the moment you are born and leave the safety and comfort of your mother's womb.

Anything you grow attached to, you can lose. Those who are interested in spirituality know that when it comes to topics such as grief, saying goodbye, and letting go, the lessons are not hard to grasp intellectually. Things become a lot harder when you try to apply that knowledge to your heart. Let me phrase that in a more concrete way: You can understand that the pain you experience is caused by your resistance to what is, but that doesn't make it any less f*cked. It's the essence of Buddhism: The cause of our suffering is desire, and nirvana is detachment from those desires. Our pain is caused by our own thoughts and actions. Everything is transient, so being enlightened implies that you fully surrender to that impermanence.

If you want to look at it this way, grief could be one of the least "spiritual" emotions you could experience. But to make the case for a life in which we accept and adjust to what is, I'd also like to argue that all emotions have a right to exist—grief too. Grief has a bittersweet beauty to it: When you become aware of the impermanence of things, you also become aware of the value and beauty of the moment. Accepting that nothing is permanent is the perfect landing strip for the present moment. Grief itself is also moving. Grief comes and goes. Grief is, like your bad days, a dialogue with life. It can offer you a master class in self-knowledge and resilience.

The Five Stages of Grief
for Bad Days

◇◇◇◇◇◇◇◇◇◇◇◇◇◇◇◇

When you're mourning a loss, whether big or small, sooner or later someone will point you to Elisabeth Kübler-Ross's five stages of grief. But grief is not a step-by-step plan; it's more of a liquid whole. It can feel as though you're inside a pinball machine with these five phases, bouncing back and forth between them. Still, knowing and recognizing the five stages can offer helpful guidance.

1. Anger

This is your "What the fuck!" response. *Why do I have to go through this? What is life doing to me?* This is the stage when you want to smash things, want to hit someone, when you might be looking for a scapegoat. Unreasonableness is your best friend at this stage, perhaps together with mild aggression. These are not welcome emotions; they run counter to self-control and decency, which we value highly in our culture. But anger is an emotion from your basic toolkit, and it can easily be aimed at something. Anger is like the element of fire: You can make it flare up high, but it's best to do it in a somewhat controlled way; otherwise, your anger may cause irreparable damage. Pick an endurance sport, get in the boxing ring, or find some other outlet. I always find my car an excellent place to curse at the top of my lungs.

2. Bargaining

This is the stage in which you want to negotiate the circumstances. You're not giving up yet. This isn't game over. There's an emerging energy that spurs you into action. You want to push boundaries, set yourself goals, all in a brave attempt to take fate back into your own hands. People who are grieving can make big decisions based on this emotion; they can go through major lifestyle changes, such as quitting their job, changing their diet, or starting a new sport. Or they can make resolutions to, for example, "never drink again" or "always say yes." It's an "if, then . . ." negotiation. You are trying to regain your security with the same force with which it was taken from you.

3. Denial

No, our relationship isn't over at all; we're only giving each other some space. Or: *Tomorrow everything will be back to normal.* It's listed as the third stage, but denial is often the first impulse after a loss. It's actually a very sweet mechanism our brain uses to try to protect us from a painful truth that is perhaps larger than we are able to grasp. When, often unconsciously, you refuse to face the truth, you can continue to carry on for a little while—on autopilot, if need be. Survival comes first. Children do this when they're confronted with news they can't immediately process: They blink their eyes a couple of times and keep on playing. Later that evening, they'll suddenly burst into tears. Sometimes reality doesn't hit you all at once.

4. Depression

And then comes the realization that it actually is true. And that nothing more can be done: no screaming, no fighting, no denial. Everything leads toward the same conclusion: the present reality is as it stands. It's a feeling of powerlessness. And feeling helpless is terrible. I know what I'm talking about. Sadness has many faces: Some people retreat into themselves and become apathetic and almost impossible to reach. Others become hysterical and start spinning. Often the new grief invokes an old grief.

5. Acceptance

Acceptance is sometimes also called adaptation: It isn't that you accept what has happened but that you begin to reorganize around your grief. A sort of acquiescence sets in. Sometimes you get to this stage quickly, and sometimes you have to wait a long time for it. I always imagine my own mourning processes as taking place in a tiny laboratory where I stop by now and again to see how things are going. One sorrow has evaporated, another is still bubbling, and that mourning over there can perhaps be moved to a back burner.

// Healthy Egotism

Feel free to prioritize yourself

You don't have to have low self-esteem or be a people pleaser to admit that it isn't always so easy to give priority to yourself over what the world asks, demands, and wants from you. It's amazing how often we are willing to do something for someone else that we deny ourselves with the greatest ease. I myself do this even with the most basic, practical things: taking the time to cook a healthy meal for others but munching on crackers with hummus when I'm by myself. Or listening to a friend for hours when I actually had planned an evening of "me time."

Life is a matter of give-and-take. Only taking isn't very chic and certainly not a sign of greatness. But just *giving*, however altruistic or "good" it may sound, isn't a sign of greatness either. When saying yes to someone else means saying no to yourself, that's something to at least be aware of. It's wonderful to be open, approachable, generous, and helpful. But if that is predominantly how others see you and you never receive anything in return, you are no more than a living hologram: a projection. Such a life is just as vain and unsteady and, in the end, empty as that of an egotist.

It seems nice, being a pleaser. *Look at me. I'm willing to do anything for others!* But make no mistake, this is another form of egotism. Often, it's a way to make you feel indispensable, or to solicit compliments, which are a fantastic fix for the ego. We can become addicted to these booster shots.

But ask yourself whether you actually are doing others a favor. Maybe your actions are denying others the chance to come up with their own solution. Besides, are you able to love yourself without that feeling that others need you? Is there enough left over for you? An unhealthy egotist doesn't just take excessively but can also be someone who gives excessively. Healthy egotists *also* derive satisfaction from taking care of themselves.

Healthy egotism also has to do with self-love and self-compassion. These terms are inextricably connected. You have to find yourself worthwhile in the same way you find others worthwhile. Positive, protective self-interest starts with the conviction that you deserve just as much as anyone else. No more, no less. Just as much. It's the knowledge that you matter, and that your contributions matter.

Giving yourself the space and grace to value yourself exactly as you are isn't easy, and it's doubly hard on bad days, when your inner critic may be screaming in your ear about what is wrong with you and your life. If this voice chimes in, stand up for yourself. Defend yourself and comfort yourself as you would defend your friends. If you can be kind to yourself and take care of yourself, you will be an example to others—even if this means not joining someone for a drink because you are exhausted. Perhaps that friend didn't really feel like going out either.

Healthy self-centeredness is an art that requires positive, honest, and constructive thoughts about who you are and what you are busy doing. One of the simplest ways to practice this is to take a step back and see yourself as your own most precious friend. How would you take care of that friend? What would you say to them? An "Are you sure you should do that?" you can imagine asking someone else is also an "Am I sure I should do this?" you should ask yourself.

Closely examine your motivation for doing or not doing something. Why you are considerate to others. Or what you consistently choose for yourself. Are your decisions or behavior motivated by love or by fear? Do you feel you deserve more or less than others? Should you be compensated for something? Are you afraid of missing out or getting shortchanged? These questions may not yield pleasant answers, but if you are able to be honest with yourself, you will create space for something lighter.

Self-love and self-compassion lower stress levels, reduce the negativity in your life, and increase your chances of gaining success, happiness, and a sense of inner peace. You don't need to always formulate exactly why you are making a certain decision. Sometimes an intuitive impulse is enough. Just ensure that the decision to do something for someone else is just as good and natural an opportunity to do something for yourself. Your intuition can function perfectly as a measuring instrument for this: Often you've already sensed what is right and it all comes down to courage. And if you can't get a good sense of what you want, if you cannot reach that pure knowing, then examine which people, situations, or convictions are causing static on the line.

And, yes, it's freakin' difficult to do this in practice. Not only because you have to deal with the possible reactions of others (you won't be surprised to know that if you stop people pleasing, people won't be pleased!), but also with your own criticism and fears: *I have to do this, otherwise no one will. I shouldn't do this, because otherwise he/she will stop loving me.*

Finally, here's a perhaps painful reality, but perhaps also a great relief: You are not that important. Whatever choice you make, most likely the world will continue to spin, and everyday life will envelop the consequences of your decision like spray foam, as if there had never been room for other options. In most cases, the well-being of humanity doesn't rest on your shoulders. The universe can be quite indifferent to everyday worries that to you may seem Very Important. In the grand scheme of things, they are totally insignificant. Reminding yourself of that can really put things in perspective.

// Choice Overload

When you don't know anymore

Never do something you don't want to do. It's one of those dime-a-dozen bits of life advice that sounds rational and lovely but ultimately makes me want to tear my hair out. Not everything in life is a choice you can address with a simple "yes, please" or "no, thank you." There's a kind of bottom line, where things sometimes just are *imperative*, whether you feel like it or not. Even not choosing is a choice. In practice, this adage is about something else: owning your choices. Knowing what you do and why, and then just *doing* it.

A recent cover of *O, The Oprah Magazine* read "What do you stand up for?" A friend from Los Angeles sent it to me because it was such a powerful question. What *do* I stand for? What do I fight for? You know, deep down, that certain things in life are so pure and true that you are willing to *stand up* for them. Once you know for yourself what these things are, the choice overload becomes a little lighter. Every choice you make will either bring you something or take something away. It's up to you to guard that equilibrium.

Nobody chooses pain, sickness, or hardship. Nevertheless, you show up for those challenges because they make an appeal to deeper values like compassion, self-care, and balance. Sometimes you have to do things that are sad or painful. And, to be clear, you always have the option to run away. You could move to the other end of the world. But when faced with a choice, it's often quite clear what needs to be done. In choices, it's often really about what you want as much as it is about acceptance.

Choice overload can also be about options over which you have more control: whether or not to quit your job, start a relationship, or cut your hair. The same idea applies: Knowing *why* you do something can remove a lot of noise from your mind. Perhaps you have a silly job, but you are earning money to make that big trip. And you can say, "Never do something you don't feel like doing," but what's the point? It's more constructive to criticize the choices you make and to stop complaining about them. What's the bigger plan? Does it help you achieve your higher goals? If so, do it. Is it not profitable for you—in fuel, energy, satisfaction, personal growth, or a new perspective? Then don't do it. Make a choice.

106

When it comes down to it, there are really ever only two choices: the ego choice and the soul choice. The difference is the feeling of tension and of release. An ego choice feels hot, hasty, and impatient. I want this! And the result of your choice is never actually good enough. A soul choice feels grounded, wholesome, truthful. It's a choice you can live with, even if things turn out differently. An ego choice is an *interpretation* of what you feel, while a soul choice is rooted in *knowing* what you feel.

If you're not completely certain about a choice you need to make, write it down and put it under your pillow. Be confident that your intuition will do its work to weigh ego against soul and logic against emotion. Taking the time to do this will spare you a lot of needlessly wasted energy. At some point, suddenly, you will know it, very certainly, and on a very deep level. Take all the time you need.

What to Think about
When You Have to Make a Choice

◇◇◇◇◇◇◇◇◇◇◇◇

When I say no, what am I saying yes to? When I say yes, what am I saying no to?

Where do I see myself in five years? Will this bring me closer? Knowing what you *do* want is always more constructive than knowing what you *don't* want.

Make your choices from strength, not weakness. From love, not fear. From soul, not ego. You know what I mean. You know how that feels. If you don't, practice how that feels.

Make a list of your core values, the things you want to stand up for. For example: connection, compassion, rest, or celebration. Pick a few, five at most, write them down, and hang the list on your mirror. Each time you're facing a big choice, grab the list, and let what you find most important in your life inform your decision.

Put it under your pillow. Literally. Write it down, sleep on it, and let your subconscious mind do its work. See if you can let what you *really* want come to the surface.

Stand up for what you choose. We make decisions based on what we know now, in exactly this moment. Even if you have remorse later, you'll know you did your best. You don't have a crystal ball (and if you do, can I take a look?).

// #NoRegrets Should Be Banned

"I don't regret anything," some people say, or, "Life's too short for regret." Mwah. I don't think those people are most people. I'm also not a fan of hashtags like #noregrets. Now, I'm not one for whom regret and shame and other negative emotions have no place. After all, I prefer to lead an inclusive life, one that has a place for all emotions, including ugly ones and raw ones. And regret is such a meaningful emotion; it mirrors with absolute clarity where you were living beyond yourself.

Whenever I hear people saying that they regret nothing or that, as Charlotte Brontë said so well, remorse is the poison of life, my face twitches. To me, saying that you never have regrets sounds like a coat of armor: *Everything I do is just and infallible—no room for discussion.* I always secretly hope that people who claim to never have any regrets actually mean something different and that maybe what they actually mean is: *I don't feel any regret anymore because I'm willing to accept the lessons that life is presenting to me. I'm familiar with those feelings of regret, but I'm not lingering in them. I accept them and live with how things went, even if I maybe wished things had gone differently.*

Regret, in its purest form, points you to an alternative possibility. It's like shining one of those blue CSI lights on your life. Regret will illuminate things you did or said (or didn't do or say) that don't fully align with who you want to be or what you want in this life.

I almost cannot imagine never experiencing regret. There are so many things I regret. Regrets are the little levees that have been built in the river of my life, that changed the water's flow. Having no regrets means not learning from your experiences. Regret pushes us back in the right direction. Maya Angelou said it beautifully: "Do the best you can until you know better. Then when you know better, do better." Those words only have meaning if you're willing to cross the quicksand of regret once in a while. That burning feeling and those red cheeks are the flashing lights indicating choices that shouldn't be repeated. When you went against yourself, often against your better judgment. When desire and expectations, insecurity or recklessness won.

Regret is a bitter pill to swallow. And regret often goes together with shame, or anger, or a feeling of injustice. "If only I had . . ." Yes, *if only*. But you chose differently. To quote Pema Chödrön again: "Nothing disappears until it has taught us what we need to know." That's what I mean about quicksand: If you resist, you will surely not get out. But learn to see regret as an invitation to transformation, to change, and the taste of an experience will shift from bitter to bittersweet. I'm sorry, and it's okay. Start healing. When you forgive yourself or others, you create space in which you can move forward.

Did you know that most people feel greater regret about what they didn't do than about what they did do? Often, regret is no more than a hangover from a choice that wasn't right, something you denied or didn't allow yourself. Often, regret can be prevented, by learning how to make "front end" decisions that are better aligned with what you want or desire. Life constantly offers new chances and new opportunities. Learn from your regret. Tune in to your body, your mind, and your intuition on a deeper level, and allow them to do their work, unhurried, unforced. The more you dare to welcome regret as a teacher, the less you may experience it going forward, because you're learning lessons. And because subsequently, wiser and more experienced, you again make a choice, you'll be able to wear that choice unapologetically, even if it didn't pan out as you expected. Because you were there. Present and able.

// **Apologies and Forgiveness**

What if you regret things, words, actions, or convictions that you wish you'd said, done, or thought differently, better, or more honestly? "Sorry" seems to be the hardest word . . . But is saying you're sorry really a sign of weakness? I'm quite certain it isn't. In my opinion, saying you're sorry and forgiving has little to do with servile humility, and more with owning the choices you've made. With a little luck, you can learn something about yourself, and something will be set in motion. Only then will the mistakes or the unfortunate decisions you made turn into learning moments when you can allow yourself to reflect on them and when you start taking your own responsibility as seriously as the outside factors. Besides, sometimes something needs to be forgiven. And sometimes you yourself are the one in need of forgiveness.

The antidote to regret is (self-)compassion, from which forgiveness flows. Withheld apologies are like splinters of curdled emotion in your inner peace. The only way to get rid of them is to pull them out in one fell swoop. Just say you are sorry. Allow remorse. Learn from it. Then move on. Forgiving is one of the hardest things there is, I do know that. It's a nice topic to read about, but in practice, it's heavy stuff. To sincerely forgive and to sincerely ask for forgiveness are serious business.

Am I good at saying I'm sorry? Yes, pretty good. For me, it doesn't require an enormous ego struggle to acknowledge my own role in matters. Am I good at forgiving? No, not always. Especially not on bad days. There still are people in my life in whose presence the words "I forgive you" don't roll off my tongue in the zen, enlightened, compassionate way I aspire to. And when it comes to some of my personal choices, getting from remorse to forgiveness isn't always a walk in the park. To forgive because you have to is useless anyway. You can't force the moment; for it to be genuine, it will be the result of a process.

What I *have* been succeeding at more quickly, more often, and with more ease, however (meditation *does* pay off!), is forgiving the situation. It feels like this: acknowledging that there is no guilt, but rather inability. That things simply happened this way, without bad intentions or deliberate cruelty. To be able to sincerely say, "It is what it is"—and not in an indifferent, "whatever" way.

By the way, once you are ready, you should know that sincerely apologizing out loud or voicing regret really is much less difficult than you might expect. The embarrassment or pain you think you will feel, the anticipation, is far more complicated and energy-draining than the act itself. It's like jumping into cold water: Just do it, because all that tiptoeing around the water's edge will make you colder than the plunge itself. You've probably seen someone else doing it and felt the urge to just scream: "For the love of God, just say you're *sorry* already! Get over yourself!"

Forgiveness comes in many different shapes and sizes. Forgiving someone who didn't show up for your birthday party is of a different order from forgiving someone who severely breached your trust. Forgiving yourself for binge-eating three Kit Kat bars is not the same as forgiving yourself for knowingly failing yourself.

A possible consolation? Forgiving something is not the same as saying you approve of it. In the end, it has more to do with the awareness that the other person is human, and that you are human, with all the imperfection that entails. Nobody is wholly good, nor bad through and through. We all want to experience love, to be safe, to survive. In *that* we are one. Saying you're sorry and being able to forgive takes you to a deeper level, a place where your ego isn't just hurt and offended, but also a place of love and unity. And there you'll also find a place to heal.

Forgiveness isn't something you do (just) for the other person; you do it for yourself. You cut the threads tying you to a negative energy. Saying "I forgive you, I no longer hold it against you" is a work in progress. Forgiveness breathes in, and out. Feel free to first be obstinate, angry, resentful, or crass, if that's what is necessary. Still, it will make your days lighter if you manage to restore the balance.

Saying You're Sorry

◇◇◇◇◇◇◇◇◇◇◇◇◇

Practice what you would like to say. Let your regrets find a form in language. Start with "I'm sorry about that," and then try to make a concrete statement of what you're sorry about. Don't omit painful details. And do this for and against yourself.

Pick your moment. Sometimes things have to calm down first. The best time to say you're sorry is when you sincerely experience—honestly, empathetically, and purely—that you have done something wrong.

Be sincere. Not ready to apologize without making excuses? Then don't do it. Saying you're sorry just to say it is pointless and, at best, a way to relieve some tension. A proper apology is not followed by a "but . . ."

Apologize without expectations. Be selfless. Offer your apologies; place them in front of you. It is up to the other person to accept or reject them, and you have no influence over their decision. Realize that in advance: Saying you're sorry is where it ends for you and where it starts for the other person. Yes, it would be nice if it could be an equal transaction, but you can only take responsibility for your own part.

Listen to what the other person has to say. You don't have to deal with it right away, but you do need to respect their emotions and perspective.

Sometimes you don't get the chance to say you're sorry in person. If so, practice forgiveness from within, and let it flow out into the world. Do little things to show that you have sincerely forgiven: You no longer talk badly about the person, you can reflect on the person or situation without judgment or expectations, you can examine your own role and can honestly say that the incident or situation is archived.

Spare others the enlightened version of yourself. Nothing is more painful than a superior attitude from which you generously grant others forgiveness. Yuck. Be humble, human, and relatable. Don't turn forgiveness into a form of ego theater.

// **Perhaps a Coach After All**

Getting help from a pro isn't that crazy

To me it's a mystery why, when we visit the dentist twice a year, regularly get our breasts and wombs checked for unwanted "activity," take our cars in for an annual service check, slather ourselves with sunscreen, and regularly have our eyes examined, we aren't regularly seeking an expert opinion of our psychological and spiritual well-being. What's the status? What is going well, what needs improvement?

In the old days, people were likely receiving these checkups from their tribe or their church elders, but those traditional structures are long gone. Fortunately, there's something called coaching. During certain moments in my life, coaching has been very reflective, forming, and empowering; if it were up to me, I would have it codified as a basic human right. I suspect I've done a great service to the Dutch coaching guild: I've pointed many a friend who threw their hands up to heaven in despair to an earthly alternative, something closer to home: coaching.

To me, visiting a coach is like cleaning out a closet: You pull everything from the coat hangers; turn the drawers upside down; check what still fits you, what has worn out, what to discard or wash; and then fold, place, and hang everything back where it belongs in an orderly fashion. If your head feels like an overstuffed, dusty, disorganized closet full of thoughts, then coaching might be just what the doctor ordered.

A coach is different from a psychologist. Psychologists are behavioral experts and offer targeted therapy. If you are experiencing a mental health crisis or want to unpack the root cause of a particular past behavior, a psychologist is a good choice. A coach is more focused on practical matters, on solutions. A coach will likely start from what is and primarily looks at the future. A coach can help you find more flexibility and clarity so you can achieve your goals, no matter how large or small. Coaching tends to focus on exploring who you are and what you wish to accomplish; it helps with self-awareness and personal growth.

Let's be honest: Not all coaches are created equal, and it's not a regulated profession. Anyone can call themselves a coach—no education or experience needed. Therefore you may, and should, be critical about who you allow to coach you. It has to feel really good. Nobody is perfect, but it's nice if the person you consult has done their homework. A good coach doesn't respond from his or her own old pain and patterns, but is at your service. A good coach is able to get the best out of your self-reflecting ability. They don't offer exuberant consolation, intensely sympathize, know better, shower you in random spiritual one-liners that aren't really that relevant to the things you're struggling with. Good coaches don't laugh off things, point fingers, or judge. They make sure you will get an increasingly deep understanding of who you are and how you can flourish.

And this is of the utmost importance: Your best friend or partner cannot also be your coach. In a pure coaching relationship, there's no mutual interest. You pay for what you receive, and that's it. It is so helpful and completely transparent to lay bare your soul—unimpeded, unjudged, and unabashed—to someone who professionally listens and urges you on. At times, we all need someone like that. Not because we are weak but because we sometimes need a sparring partner. A good coach gives you a little push in the right direction, so that you can continue. On a bad day, you could do with a little push like that every so often.

SHIT

does not have to
MAKE SENSE

THE
BIG BAD
WORLD
OUT
THERE

// **Dealing with External Hassle**

Wouldn't life be much, much easier if you weren't dealing with the big bad outside world? Man, how annoying to be ricocheting back and forth in the pinball machine of life. The one time I want to exercise, the gym happens to be closed for renovation. The one morning I want to sleep in, the neighbors start doing home improvements. When I happen to respond in a totally zen and calm way for once, the other person acts unreasonable. *I'm actually totally okay! It's just that the outside world is thwarting me all the time!*

Often the big bad world out there is a cause of bad days and lesser moments. Maybe you can relate to the following statements:

- I did everything I could.
- If it weren't for other people being so difficult, then . . .
- I have no control over it.
- If they hadn't interfered, then . . .
- I am not being heard anyway.
- Why do I have to worry about that?
- Why am I not being taken into account?
- It is not my fault that . . .
- I didn't do anything wrong; *they* made mistakes.
- And now I have to solve things, or make up, or sort it out again.
- They are out to undermine me.
- I'm done with it, or I'm breaking up, or I'm quitting.
- You know what—never mind. You figure it out.

This list could be much, *much* longer. What these thoughts have in common is that they point to other people. It's part of a lesser day experience to point to the big bad outside world, because on lesser days it is very tempting to find other people stupider, meaner, and less enlightened than yourself. A boomerang must always be thrown with force, but unfortunately, it will come flying back just as fast. It's generally pretty senseless to point to other people on lesser days, simply because you don't have that much influence over what's going on around you. You can't change the direction of the wind, just the position of your sails, remember?

118

Anger is a powerful energy that makes you strong and combative. It helps you to set your boundaries and not be swayed by lesser alternatives. You can wander in the Valley of Reproach for quite a long time if you feel like it, although that tends to be not very useful. Often we just do it because we don't know what else to do, or because we don't feel like taking responsibility. At some point, you have to transform anger to let it go.

You can ask yourself questions, such as: What can I do to at least improve the situation for myself? Do I have to set boundaries? Can I find a glimmer of compassion in myself and also direct it to others or to the circumstances? Is my frustration an excuse not to do, or not to eschew, something? Do I have to deal with it right *now*, or can I just let it go? What could I do differently myself? Does it change anything in the circumstances when I start to stack emotions (for example, feeling rotten about having a rotten feeling), or is this bad day bad enough without piling on? What can I do right *now* that would contribute to a slightly less grumpy, dejected, gray version of myself, independent from the big bad world out there?

// And What Does This Say about You?

In kindergarten, I learned a children's song, and I still remember the first lines. It goes like this: "Take a look around you, just take a look. Take someone else's hand, for you are not alone. Together we can have fun, sing, and play. We may be small, but playing together makes a great day." I still think these words are lovely. You're not alone in this world. Now that's a sweet reminder for a lesser day, isn't it?

But no matter how spiritually ideal it may be, the fact that someone lives a conscious life doesn't automatically make them everyone's friend. Let's not be holier-than-thou. You can't fool me that you like to spend your free time with that nosy, nose-picking toddler on the third floor, with your sighing and whimpering ex, or with that woman who tests that sound barrier with her shrill, fake laugh at every party. Providing other people with love, happiness, and a sense of safety isn't necessarily the same as hanging on the couch with them until all the wine runs out. We can pretend otherwise, but we're talking real life here.

Especially on tough days, it can be a wise decision to close yourself off from other people's energy when the vibes aren't charging you positively. Go and sit inside your cocoon, if need be. But when others are causing your bad days or making them worse, it can be interesting to ask yourself why you let your environment get under your skin like that. It may be a cliché of the first order, but being irritated by or disliking someone oftentimes says something about you as well. Apparently, that person triggers a sense of aversion in you. That's annoying to hear because it's so much more convenient to point to others; however, it'd only be fair to admit it if it's true, because with such honesty, you can create space and distance for yourself, give yourself a little more air, and draw off some of the tension you feel.

You can learn something from everyone you meet. Really. And by that I mean literally everyone you ever met or will ever meet. Other people are a perfect mirror for what you're transmitting. There are spiritual schools that assume that anyone crossing your path enters your life with a purpose. I'm not sure how literally you should take this "path crossing"—I always think: Well, that would turn a rush-hour subway trip into a very intense ride. But it is certainly fascinating to ponder how you can use your interaction with other people as a crash course in self-knowledge.

EVELINE HELMINK

The trick, of course, is to discover *what* it is exactly that you can learn from others. And to do that, a question was conceived that is often used in a slightly passive-aggressive manner: "So, what does this actually say about you?" I'd like to advise against using this question as a trump card in pseudo-therapeutic settings or heated arguments, but, in essence, it's a good question. What *does* your feeling of irritation, admiration, love, fear, panic, or jealousy say about you? What was it in a given encounter that provoked this reaction or emotion? Is there something you perhaps would like to be able to do? Or be? For example, I have a mild allergy to people who always complain about their health, but that most likely says something about my own inability to be a little less stern now and then when it comes to my own well-being.

On bad days, try not to focus all your attention on other people. Occasionally, dare to ask yourself: Is there something to be learned here about who I am and what I think is important? Would this be a moment for me to practice my loving-kindness and compassion?

First Aid for
Energy Vampires

◇◇◇◇◇◇◇◇◇◇◇◇◇◇

We deal with other people all day, every day. That's just how it is, whether offline or online, far away or up close. When you detect energy vampires in your direct environment, try to consciously isolate yourself from them. Don't meet up with that friend for a while, the one from whom you always come home exhausted. See if you can change the way you work with that particular colleague. Don't pick up the phone for a while. Leave the curtains closed for a day, if you feel you need it. Sometimes you just have to. And the outside world will just have to deal with it.

A nice visualization technique is that of a golden egg. When you quickly need something—say, you're about to enter a room or meet someone—take a couple of minutes to visualize a thin, golden, and unbreakable skin around you that can only be penetrated by positive vibes. Inside this egg, you are safe and protected. "Whoa, she's saying that I have to imagine a golden egg around myself?" Yup. And it works, I promise.

// The Lives You Don't Lead

When I discovered the meaning of "sonder"

I've always been fascinated with the idea of the lives one is not living. Maybe this rings a bell for you. It's something most of us have experienced as children—amazement about just how big the world is, and everything one can become and experience. Some adults still have it, by the way. I spent a sleepless night after I first learned about parallel universes, in which your alternative lives play out in infinite parallel bubbles. Each time you take a right turn, you also turn left, resulting in a new bubble. With every choice we make, we simultaneously don't make one. For each turn we take, we're missing another one. In the multiverse, however, you're living each and every one of them! With Stephen Hawking's theories in mind, you'll never look at bath soap the same way.

So there are an infinite number of lives you are not living and countless lives you *could've* had—if you'd chosen a different major, had stayed with her, had boarded that plane anyway. On bad days, these aren't necessarily the most pleasant scenarios to play out in your mind. "Had I . . ." The less you feel at home in your own life, the greater the desire for everything to be different.

Yet there's also a wonderful side to being aware of the lives you're not leading. It may remind you of the things you truly find important—perhaps not necessarily how an endeavor would have worked out in practice, but the values you put into it. It's possible that you didn't want to live in rural Tanzania per se, but that you did long to live closer to nature. Maybe it's perfectly fine that you didn't become a professional dancer, but that doesn't mean that dancing can't give you a good feeling anymore. On the one hand, accepting your life course is an exercise in surrender; on the other, it's a useful compass.

One of the most comforting thoughts there is, I find, is that your life—however boring, stupid, insignificant, or ugly it may seem for the moment—is *your* life. And that . . . that is *enough*. It is a life worth living. Everyone has their own, unique story, and that's precisely what connects us all. The basic ingredients are pretty much almost always the same: love, hope, desire, headwind, tailwind. Knowing that you are but a knot in a gigantic cosmic tapestry, which could've been somewhere else without disrupting the pattern, has something immensely consoling about it.

Do you know the word "sonder" and what it means? I learned about it by listening to the podcast *S-Town*, a beautiful documentary about the life of a unique man who, without this podcast, would've probably remained pretty much unknown. "Sonder" is the realization that each random person is leading a life that is just as vivid and complex as your own—filled with their own ambitions, friends, routines, worries, and folly. We owe this marvelous word to John Koenig, the man behind the amazing project *The Dictionary of Obscure Sorrows*. Koenig coins words for emotions for which existing language comes up short, with the goal of helping us better understand each other and making us aware of our enormous emotional palette. If you haven't seen his TED Talk, I highly recommend that you do so.

Realizing that each of us is leading a life that is worth living, no matter what, makes you feel connected to other people. You play a part in many different narratives, likely without being aware of it. Whenever you feel small, insignificant, and measly, let this be somewhat of a consolation. You're living a life, and it is a unique life.

EVELINE HELMINK

// Social Media Detox

Don't swipe yourself a depression

I'm not someone who sees the devil's hand in social media. I don't believe "likes" will be the downfall of civilization. Thanks to social media, I've gotten to know amazing people, found inspiration, discovered new teachers, and ended up in places I wouldn't have known otherwise. For example, I once roamed Tokyo for a day with a Brazilian-Japanese girl who had announced, via a message on Instagram, that she was reading the international edition of *Happinez*. We ate at local spots with her friends, and she showed me around temples where I would've never ended up as a tourist.

But social media is downright bad when things aren't going well for you. Everyone seems happier, more organized, fitter, younger, hipper, more successful, and smarter on the days when you don't feel that way about yourself. In addition, social media also has the power to turn everything into cookie-cutter uniformity: How many people can possibly love brass palm tree hooks, pink velour sofas, green hanging plants, and red-and-white-checked Ibiza dresses?

If you're not in top form, your soul can short-circuit with too much social media. Our soul isn't made to blend into the crowd, and social media can lead you jarringly far away from your originality, from what *you* find beautiful, from what truly is a part of you. On a bad day, this happens ten times faster. You lose yourself, and that always feels terrible.

When I notice that social media is starting to annoy me or suck up my time, an alarm bell goes off in my head. I too have days when I hang on the couch, phone in hand, and swipe, swipe, swipe. Not many things are as time killing and soul crushing as scrolling and swiping: Suddenly it's 10:30 a.m., and I haven't eaten or done anything. Social media platforms seem custom-engineered for bad days: They offer a mix of effortless, repetitive action and constant, tiny pleasure shots, perfectly blended to lull your mind into a state of half slumber, one that doesn't feel like waking or sleeping. In other words, a drug. Sedation for your lesser days.

The effect of social media on our brain is still being researched; online terms such as "Snapcrack" and "Instagrams" are being thrown around. Social media sites appear to micro-dose us with little fixes, like other drugs, stimulating our brains to produce dopamine.

In 2014, I attended a Wisdom 2.0 conference, a meeting in San Francisco about conscious living in the modern age, at which teachers like Jon Kabat-Zinn and Byron Katie shared a stage with engineers and CEOs from tech firms like Google and Facebook. *The* topic of conversation was how we've manipulated our minds. And sure, you might just find that one uplifting quote or funny picture that drags you out of your inertia, but let's be brutally honest: Using your smartphone for answers in an absentminded state is worse than looking for a needle in a haystack. You have to scroll through 574 photos before finally getting your shot.

So however hard it may be on a bad day, pull the plug. Put that thing aside. Seek out places to be unplugged, or create one for yourself. In the time you save, you can start liking your own thoughts for a change. Perhaps it's time to determine your self-worth, without your ego's subconscious tricks and the parameters of others with their amazing homes, new lovers, and cool jobs. Social media sessions are binge fests for egos that love comparison and belonging, that thrive on attention, confirmation, novelty, and contact.

If you can resist the temptation to binge? You'll have spare time, vast oceans of hours you can devote to things that actually are good for you. Like sleeping. Conversations with real people. Exercise. My most relaxed vacations were those when I stayed somewhere with super crappy Wi-Fi. After the first twenty-four hours of shock, it was a gift from heaven. You can stand under that waterfall without trying to add a catchy caption in your head. And you can free yourself from knowing whether the world is on fire, because there's nothing you could be doing about it anyway.

Bad Days vs. Social Media

◇◇◇◇◇◇◇◇◇◇◇◇◇◇◇

If you recognize some of these statements, maybe you should put your phone away:

- *You think "Why don't I have that?" instead of "Good for them!"*
- *You feel the need to spruce up your own reality.*
- *You regularly check how many followers others have.*
- *You keep hitting "refresh" to see your likes increase.*
- *You think you've put up a unique picture, but stuff others are posting is almost identical.*

To reduce the time you spend scrolling, try some of these tips:

- *Turn off your notifications.* Don't be pushed.
- *Do not use the apps;* instead, use the desktop versions of Instagram, etc., if possible.
- *Set a timer* on your Wi-Fi.
- *Place your phone* in another room.
- *Unsubscribe from 90 percent* of your newsletters.
- *Do not open your social media* until you are up and running or already winding down after a long day.
- *Keep track of how much time* you spend on social media for a week, and think about what you actually could do with that time.
- *Unfollow, unfriend, or mute people* whose contributions don't bring you anything. Dare to be picky, and consider what you want to spend your precious attention on.
- *Choose which social media platform suits you best,* and leave the others for what they are. (I deleted my Twitter account years ago, because it does not suit me.)
- *Consider what you do want,* and strategically use social media for that purpose alone.
- *Choose a few topics* for which you want to find inspiration or motivation, and focus on those for a while. Unfollow when you are satisfied or have moved on. When I was moving, I followed a lot of interior décor and style accounts. Now that my house is more or less finished, these just make me greedy; following them no longer serves me in a positive way.

// **Turn Off the News**

Make your world small

We are living in an era of abundance and of being always and constantly on—not abundance of everything and not everybody is always on, but generally it's the state of our current culture. We have access to a limitless selection of chocolate spreads, sock colors, toothbrushes, bike bells. The same applies to information. Media-wise, in all possible ways, in all possible forms, colors, and languages, news stimuli are flowing into our heads: through social media, the radio, news tickers, screens. Whatever is happening in the world, it's coming to you.

I've been a news addict for a long time. I pride myself on reading a lot of newspapers and magazines, keeping an ear to the ground at all times, and scouring the internet for intelligent reviews, columns, and podcasts. I have a background in journalism, and I often joke that what I really have is a degree in curiosity. Though I never worked for a newscast or news medium, I find those news stimuli wonderful.

And I should confess that the tabloids were also part of my regular roundup. Some people smoke, some drink coffee, some people get their quick news fix—I'm among the latter. Opening up my search engine and . . . just a quick peek to see what's going on in the world, as well as with Beyoncé and the entire British royal family. At some point, the news turned into the background noise of my life. I checked it when I woke up in the morning and late at night before falling asleep.

I've heard that of the thousands of news stories you consume annually, only a few are truly relevant for your own personal life. Each day, there are countless events taking place, but the chance that one of them happens to you or has an impact on you doesn't increase or decrease by you being more or less up to date on the details of all the others. What really matters will surface eventually, even if you limit your attention to set moments in the day and a handful of high-quality sources.

Only it doesn't feel like that of course. The news stimulates you and is often addictive. You are eager to know how a story develops and how it ends, and so you stay tuned. The trouble is that this can be to the detriment of your creativity and your problem-solving skills, which benefit from free space, sans distractions and preconceptions. News wakes you up, makes you alert, and gives you a sense of involvement and connection. But with what? Continuous news cycles trigger stress hormones, disrupt your concentration (and can in the long term even diminish it), and create noise in your day-to-day routine.

News is often addictive: Bad days don't benefit from news that doesn't positively contribute to your well-being. If you aren't in a great place emotionally, taking a news break is a smart idea. What good does it do you to know that, somewhere in the world, there was a mass murder or that Rihanna got a haircut? It doesn't change your life, here and now, except that it colors your day. It invokes emotions that don't belong to you and that don't benefit your here and now. It would be better to direct your energy inward, to focus on whatever news broadcasts and headlines pop up in your inner world. On bad days, I leave the world events for what they are, and invite you to do the same.

// Losing Sleep over Money

It's both important and unimportant, all at the same time

Money is a difficult subject. Talking about it is so . . . so vulgar. "Hey, it's just money!" I try to cheer myself up when I find a hefty parking ticket in the mail or when the end of the month is looking austere. And, instinctively, something as mundane and practical as money can seem far removed from matters of personal growth and inner peace.

Then again, spirituality and money have a complicated relationship, as if they're two opposites on a line between heaven and earth. To some, one's attitude toward money is a measure of enlightenment: If you worry about it, apparently your confidence isn't high enough. Afraid of scarcity? Well, that means you've got some soul crafting ahead of you. But try saying something like "Money can't buy you happiness" to a single mother on welfare. Your soul can overflow from trust in abundance all it wants, but it doesn't buy you a loaf of bread.

We have to deal with money—that's just how it is. Money is a fact of life. You need it to feed yourself and to live, if you don't have the desire for a completely alternative lifestyle. Worries about money can be a genuine cause of a bad day. Or perhaps on bad days you use your money in exchange for some soul soothing—in the form of takeout sushi, a new pair of shoes, or a random online purchase for which you just clicked "check out" without removing a single item from your loaded cart.

If, for you, money and bad days are related, it may be helpful to remember that money in and of itself is neither good nor bad. It's a tool. In essence, money is a sort of energy that's being exchanged. You do something and receive money in return, or you spend money, for which you receive something in return. Our relationship with money—good or bad—is caused by what we associate it with. If money is making you angry or sad, it usually has to do with larger issues: There's an imbalance between effort and reward, or between spending and income. Somewhere something is awry. During lesser days, you sense more acutely where exactly the balance has been lost.

Still, I know myself well enough to realize that I too harbor a fear of scarcity. Not because I couldn't live more simply—several times in my life, I've given up my financial security and luxury to follow my heart—but because I'm scared of not being able to provide my kids with security and continuity. What really matters to me has nothing to do with money, while at the same time, money enables me to live according to my core values. I don't desire abundance, but I also don't want scarcity. I want freedom. Shortage is dependence. It's complicated!

These days, I'm more or less ambivalent when it comes to money. On the one hand, I don't worry about it: I don't *need* more than I have right now; I can provide for myself and my children. On the other hand, my situation is not so carefree that I can buy and do everything I would like. It feels balanced.

That's what it comes down to—balance. Enough but not too much. I'm not interested in business spirituality or prosperity gospels that promise you can make a million in a year while working only six hours a month. (Note: Spiritual money gurus make those amounts because *you* fund them; to a certain extent, these are pyramid schemes. At the base are the "losers" who apparently weren't able to build a business from their soul.) The trick is to figure out your equilibrium. What, for you, is enough. Lynne Twist, activist and author of the book *The Soul of Money*, wrote the following: "When you let go of trying to get more of what you don't really need, it frees up oceans of energy to make a difference with what you have."

Learning to recognize that abundance and money are separate entities can help you through bad days. It may be a cliché, but it makes sense: True wealth is love, friendship, sunlight, beautiful clouds, glistening water, a horizon. Not everything of value can be monetized. Your bank statement says nothing about who you are.

Money Woes

◇◇◇◇◇◇◇◇◇◇◇◇◇◇◇◇

Is money something you struggle with on bad days? Ask yourself these questions:

How do you use money as energy? Do you use it to comfort yourself, to impress, or to distract? Or do you use it to express yourself as well as you can?

Do you dare to ask for money in return for your efforts without feeling uncomfortable about it? Do you see it as a form of reward?

What is at stake when you don't have enough money? What stories do you tell yourself about scarcity or about your self-worth when money is tight?

If you won the lottery tomorrow, what would you do? What desires come alive in those daydreams? Freedom? Travel? A career switch? Luxury and pleasure? Would it be possible to satisfy these desires in a way that doesn't involve lots of money?

Would you consider alternatives like bartering or buying and selling secondhand? You may be able to transform your personal economy by handling your cash flow differently.

Do you have a clear grasp of your finances? Do you know what is coming in and what goes out, and how you've divided your priorities between past, present, and future? Spending money isn't hard, but whether what you receive in return is of any *real* value is interesting to contemplate. Make sure you know where your money (which, in essence, is energy) is going. Check if that is where you *want* your energy to be spent, in both the short and long term.

Having clear and honest insight into your finances will have ramifications for your life as a whole. How you handle money often mirrors how you're feeling. It will give you comfort and a sense of clarity to know how the foundation of your financial behavior was laid. This doesn't necessarily mean you have to involve Excel spreadsheets; a survey of your personal finances can take various shapes. The question isn't *how* but *whether* your financial situation is transparent.

Compile a list in two columns. In the left-hand column, list all the things you spend money on; in the one on the right, write what you're *actually* buying. "Grabbing a coffee in the city" might represent "social contact." You might think of "new shoes" as "self-expression." Then make another set of lists. In the left-hand column, copy the words from the right-hand column of the first set. In the new right-hand column, come up with alternative activities or items that could yield the same result but that require a smaller or no financial investment. For example, "social contact" can also be a walk in the park, meeting in the public library, a phone chat with a friend. Manifesting, if you can, what is important and valuable to you—independent of money—will make you more creative and will expand your world.

// What's Your Panic Room?

And also some notes on the "emergency list"

If you're not feeling good on the inside, it's comforting to be in a safe and soul-soothing environment. You can always pull the covers over your head, but that will quickly become suffocating and sweaty. Instead, I recommend that you designate other, airier spaces as panic rooms. That way, you'll always have a place to go.

The comfort of a safe space probably has something to do with a childlike need for confinement. Do you remember how it felt to sit inside a blanket fort? What it was like to drape a few bedsheets over some chairs, pin them in place, and drag a bunch of pillows into your little home? An itty-bitty safe space, where you can hide as everyday life continues outside. A perfect place for sulking or for taking some alone time. The combination of a hard floor and the smell of laundry detergent is the perfume of my bad childhood days. Try finding something like that today for yourself: a tent in the middle of the living room—we adults prefer to say tepee— is something most of us encounter only while browsing Instagram.

Although many of the tips in this book are about how to find places inside yourself, it's an excellent idea to figure out an actual physical space you can retreat to in times of discomfort and adversity. What are the places where your body relaxes, your mind calms down, and life looks less complicated? Where you can lick your wounds, dry your tears, examine your feelings and thoughts in quiet and safety?

Ranking high on my list is the public library. It is quiet there, and wherever you go all over the world, library bookshelves are reassuringly the same. The people using the library are generally concentrating on reading, and there's always a place where you can hide. I never feel lonesome in a library, but I usually feel pleasantly alone and anonymous. On lesser days, I also often seek out a body of water, preferably the ocean; a vast waterscape reminds me of my place in the order of things.

But I also enjoy being stuck in traffic, my car enveloping me like a cookie jar and safe space. I love the anonymity of hotel lobbies, with their constant ebb and flow of people coming and going. I love going to a movie theater in the middle of the day and sitting in the dark by myself. I love my editorial offices and the sound of fingers typing, and the way it slowly turns quiet by the end of the workday. I love my cyclical work flow at the magazine: coming up with ideas for the new issue, making, printing, and distributing it, and starting all over again. The common denominator is places where life goes on, no matter what, where my presence is exchangeable and transient. In those situations, I feel dissolved in time, which helps me to put things in perspective and calms me.

Lastly, my home is a panic room. It's quiet, calm, and safe. My crispy white down comforter. The large windows overlooking city, water, and air.

Whenever I don't know where to begin, you can find me in those places. Compile a list of your own places. Whether it's a forest, your best friend's sofa, the gym, or the back row of a movie theater, know where you can escape to. Know where in the outside world you can find inner calm.

The Emergency List

◇◇◇◇◇◇◇◇◇◇◇◇◇

The same way you have a list of numbers hanging on your basement door or shoved in a kitchen drawer in case your boiler stops working, the power is out, or there's no water coming out of your kitchen faucet, you should have a list of things you can do in case your internal fuse box is experiencing trouble.

On my bad days, everything is stupid, everything is too much effort, everything is meh. When I'm having a bad day, my head feels like it has been stuffed with cotton. That image is not that crazy considering that your prefrontal cortex, the front part of your brain where behavior, concentration, and creativity are located, really can be overstimulated. Time and again, reversing a bad day comes down to remembering what it is that will make you feel better.

Once, I asked a friend who went through serious periods of depression—pills, psychiatrists, the whole shebang—what he did on days when sadness and pain overshadowed everything. He had made an emergency list for himself. It contained all sorts of things he knew would make him feel better: meeting a friend for drinks, running, listening to his favorite band, good coffee. Ever since, I've kept a list like that for myself. Do this, and in those moments when you can't think of anything that will make you feel better, fear not: You've already come up with a slew of ideas.

Now you want to know my list, right? Well, among other things:

- *Seeing friends:* even though I'm actually cranky and don't always feel like doing so.
- *Making plans for, and with, my children:* Happy children's faces are comfort XL.
- *Booking a massage:* Feeling and releasing tension in my body is self-care.
- *Reading, in a comfy woolen sweater, with thick socks, on a sheepskin rug:* immersing myself in a story.
- *Writing:* messing around with language and words.
- *Lying in savasana:* in other words, practicing surrender.
- *Working out:* But, to be fair, sometimes "working out" means a long walk; any form of physical exercise will do.
- *Making soup:* Gotta love comfort food.
- *Listening to some breezy, happy-go-lucky music:* Spotify playlists with names like "Lazy Sunday" or "Coffeehouse" hit the spot.
- *Browsing books,* and completely forgetting the time in a bookstore or public library.
- *Bringing some flowers home* after picking out the most beautiful ones one by one.
- *Washing my hair:* wispy hair + a bad day = recipe for disaster.
- *Putting on some nice clothes:* making an effort for myself, even and especially if I'm not planning on seeing anyone.
- *Sleeping:* going to bed on time, putting in the hours.
- *Meditating:* sitting and keeping my mouth shut.
- *A solo visit to the cinema,* where I can be anonymous and safe.
- *Visiting a thrift store:* a bit of treasure hunting, a bit of strolling around.
- *Visiting one of my other safe spaces:* see the section above.

// The Cosmic Bank Account

Being indebted to your friends

For a while, it was trendy to wear an infinity sign on a necklace or as a tattoo. You know the one: a lemniscate, the symbol in the shape of a horizontal figure eight that represents perpetual motion, no beginning and no end, always flowing, always in balance, always bending back toward the center. This symbol is the mathematical sign for infinity. It is a beautiful symbol for friendship and the intention to make it last a lifetime.

If I had to choose a logo for the bank I run together with some of my dear friends, it would be a lemniscate. In this bank, we don't exchange money or keep gold bars. It's a sort of cosmic bank account based on the idea of a perpetually flowing give-and-take. "Love is patient," the Bible wisely reminds us. "Love is kind . . . it is not self-seeking." It's true, and although it may be somewhat unusual to associate friendship and banking, I have found it useful and freeing in my own life.

Do you know what the underlying principle of insurance is? In short, it comes down to pooling risk. You sign an agreement and commit to paying regular sums of money, knowing that your money will go to support others in their time of need. In return for supporting those people, you are also entitled to compensation if or when fate turns against you.

The principle of saving? You put something aside so you won't spend it right away but will have a reserve for later. That's how you build wealth. The cosmic bank account is a metaphor for the much deeper and more intimate ebb and flow of energy and support we share. It's a commitment you make to others. In any good relationship, whether romantic or platonic, there is always a certain balance between giving and taking. This exchange of energy is important, because when there's an imbalance, when someone always takes without giving back or when someone only sends without receiving, the relationship becomes unbalanced. Sooner or later, that will cause irritation, and then you are in debt.

Because I share that bank account with friends, and because of the plain, down-to-earth language we use to discuss our emotional exchange, it's a subject we can openly talk about. That makes the relationship transparent and loving. There have been times when, for example, I just called a friend to cry, complain, or blow off steam.

There have been times when, in return, all I heard was lamenting, with me occasionally mumbling "yes," "no," and "uh-huh" while doing the dishes. That was totally okay, though. The two of us are managing each other's savings. Each of us is paying the premium for our friendship in time, attention, and an absence of judgment. Sometimes I've felt that I had a "debt" with someone—when all I'd done was talk about my own misery— and was able to settle it. The lemniscate continues.

A couple of factors are essential when creating a veritable, pure, well-balanced cosmic account with the people dear to you. Know, for example, that *equal* and *equivalent* are two different things: You don't have to trade pain with pain or a happy story with a happy story. Sometimes you just have to invest forty-five minutes of your time to listen to your friend explaining how completing a six-piece Elmo puzzle proves that her daughter is brilliant (including when the phone is handed to the toddler in question). In turn, your friend will patiently listen as you tell her your work stories, although she doesn't know your coworkers and doesn't understand the project you're so frustrated about.

Energy doesn't always come back to you in the same form you gave it. Maybe you sent your friend a card with a handwritten message and flowers that match her interior; she's more of the "actions speak louder than words" type and comes to pick you up from the airport in the middle of the night.

If you aren't sure whether your most precious friendships are balanced, "giving" is always a good starting point. Stay in contact, even if it's just a text message or a card. Be the first to say you're sorry, if apologies are needed. Offer help, even if it actually isn't your turn to do so. Giving and taking in a friendship is a complicated matter. Call the cosmic bank account by its name. It's a lighthearted way to discuss something immensely complicated.

EVERYDAY LIGHT THINGS

// Playing Creator

Go make something

You know what's good for your soul? To create. Especially on the hard days, when it may feel as if you aren't in control and when you aren't particularly buzzing with creativity, it's a perfect idea to take matters into your own hands and make something. Doesn't really matter what you make, just something. Soup. A drawing. A swing. Anything.

On Wiktionary, I happened to stumble upon the term "soulcraft." There were two definitions. The first: an activity that is nourishing to the soul, or fulfilling. The second: something that shapes and modifies one's soul or core being. When you perform such tasks, you spring into action and force your mind to concentrate. It's the magic in the repetitive motions of coloring, knitting, carving, kneading, or building that has a calming effect on you. To see something slowly emerge gives you a feeling of satisfaction. It really happens; whether you want it to or not, your body will take care of it. Making something is an excellent way to trigger a shot of dopamine that functions as an antidepressant of sorts and takes the edge off your lesser day in a natural way.

"I'm not creative"; "I'm not handy"; "I don't like crafts." Fine. But don't dismiss the concept. Creating something helps trigger your imagination while also developing your problem-solving capability, skills that might come in handy. You don't have to be extraordinarily creative to benefit from creating. You can make all sorts of things, and the process can be either moving and stunning or a useless flop. You don't have to use cheerful, bright colors. You don't have to clear out your local crafts store for supplies. Your project can be substantial—perhaps you feel like painting or working on a vision board, something like that. But it can just as well be a super workaday task like sewing on a button or making fresh pizza dough from scratch.

The secret is this: You don't have to do anything with the end product of the time you've spent creating. There's no requirement that anyone has to look at it or eat it or that you have to keep it in a place of honor on your mantel for the rest of your days. Just because you felt like painting doesn't mean you have to hang your artwork on the wall. I find it stress reducing, for example, to endlessly string beads from my niece's beads box, even though I don't really wear jewelry, much less homemade concoctions. Give your crafts away or throw them out. It doesn't matter; the important thing isn't the result.

Tibetan monks who create painstakingly detailed and labor-intensive sand mandalas simply sweep them away afterward. I have been present for one of those ceremonies, and it's wonderful and oddly freeing to witness. The magic of the mandala—so carefully designed and so perfectly balanced, so meticulously made up out of millions of grains of sand—is broken without hesitation, in one fell stroke of a broom. The underlying message: Everything is constantly in motion, nothing is permanent.

The process of creating perfect harmony and balance is primarily about mirroring the creation process *itself*, not only in its shape but also in its movement. Not being so wedded to the result—that is an interesting idea to practice when you decide to experiment with this shortcut. It will help you to let go of the goal, to experience the pleasant side effects of the creation process itself, without your ego nagging you with the question "So, is it Insta-worthy?"

Working with your hands will lighten your days, because it adds to your sense of self-worth and autonomy. We are used to being in our heads; that's where society encourages us to be. Jobs that require knowledge tend to be valued more highly than jobs that rely on the things people can do with their hands. This causes, consciously or unconsciously, an imbalance between thinking and doing. When you get your hands dirty, you can begin to balance these two elements. It connects you with the physical world—with materials, with form, with tactility. It temporarily gets you out of your head and perhaps out of the virtual world of TV and social media as well.

Knead the dough. Finish a jigsaw puzzle. Draw a mandala. Sew a sock puppet. Mend your clothes. Build a chicken coop. It's enough to be present in the process. And who knows, perhaps you will accidentally create something beautiful, after all.

// Write It Out of Your System

Paper. Pen. Go.

It probably has become clear to you that it isn't always productive to just let yourself marinate in a bad day. It's better to be in touch with your emotions, to feel them and learn from them. Maybe by now you're mildly intrigued by the fact that your days will become lighter if you manage to find an outlet for your feelings and thoughts. But perhaps you have yet to find the words. Perhaps you don't feel like having human interaction right now. If this sounds like you, praise the day that pen and paper were invented.

Writing is a powerful way to express yourself. Now, of course, our inner critic would prefer to do so in beautifully crafted sentences, heartfelt poetry, or along logically structured lines. As a journalist and magazine editor, I know what it's like to craft stories that will be read by others, how it is to work from A to Z, to delight and instruct. But what you need to do on bad days is a totally different kind of writing. It's shapeless, intimate, and pure. It's strictly about the process of searching for language, of surprising yourself with what flows from your pen. It's *play*, not work.

Writing on bad days is a particular kind of writing; it's not for a reading audience or for posterity, but is a way to arrange and deposit your thoughts. Afterward you can throw the paper in the trash, tear it into a thousand pieces, or burn it (in a responsible manner, please).

What matters is that you use your pen to download something. Thinking is fleeting: thoughts come and go, tumble over each other and evaporate, and what remains is a feeling, or an energy. Writing makes you aware of what you are thinking, and maybe also of the impact of those thoughts. When you write, you start a dialogue with yourself. Wise Raphaël Enthoven, who gives writing workshops based on the principle of "proprioceptive writing" puts it like this: "By writing, you slow down the thought process. You get to know your own way of thinking. Suddenly you see more clearly which things make you doubt, what you're afraid of, where your strengths lie and what it is you desire. That will give you a direction and something to hold on to in seemingly hopeless situations."

There are many writing methods that inspire and give direction and relief. Natalie Goldberg wrote a book called *Writing Down the Bones*, an absolute gold standard on writing as a means for personal growth and self-understanding. Goldberg says, "To begin writing from our pain eventually engenders compassion for our small and groping lives. Out of this broken state there comes a tenderness for the cement below our feet, the dried grass cracking in a terrible wind. We can touch the things around us we once thought ugly and see their special detail, the peeling paint and gray of shadows as they are—simply what they are: not bad, just part of the life around us—and love this life because it is ours and in the moment there is nothing better."

Geertje Couwenbergh, author of *Zin*, a book about inspired writing, calls pain a gatekeeper. When you write about what hurts, you will get closer to (self-)love, innocence, and consolation. "Writing, if you do it well, strips you of any urge to be different from who you are," Geertje argues. And: "Writing is a form of ultrapersonal self-examination. Pain in writing is a sign that you're getting closer to the truth. The truth of life, to be precise. That truth, as the saying goes, is liberating. Healing."

When you write, you translate a bad day into concrete words and sentences. You alleviate the traffic in your head by "parking" your thoughts in a different spot than your own mind. Did you read the Harry Potter books or perhaps see the movies? Albus Dumbledore pulls memories from his head in the form of ethereal silver threads and stores them in a special wide, shallow dish called a pensieve. When he needs the memories, he studies them, but by siphoning off his excess thoughts, he doesn't have to carry around all of his ideas and experiences with him.

But what should you write? Well, that actually isn't step one. Step one is that you begin writing at all. Julia Cameron, who wrote the classic *The Artist's Way*, advises a method known as "morning pages": Each morning she fills three white pages with anything that comes up in her mind—regardless of whether she has inspiration or not. The power lies in the rhythm, the repetition, which will lead you past the little voice in your head toward a deeper consciousness. So buy a notebook or grab one from your stack of unused beautiful ones. If you have trouble breaking in that pristine first white page, think this: If you don't write on it, you deny that page the fulfillment of its true role. That would be sad, now, wouldn't it? Well, then! Start writing.

If You Really, Truly
Have No Idea Where to Begin

◇◇◇◇◇◇◇◇◇◇◇◇◇◇◇

Set a timer. Start with twenty minutes or whatever feels comfortable, and during that time, write down whatever comes to mind, without stopping or even lifting your pen off the paper. Write down your thoughts, no matter how disjointed. Punctuation, style, and spelling are of minor concern. Keep going. If necessary, repeat your last sentence over and over until a new thought emerges.

Choose a genre or form. For example, create a third-person narrative about what you're experiencing. "Today Eveline is having a hard day. It started with an increasing irritability caused by . . ." A perspective like that creates distance. Another idea: Write a manifesto with your intentions for today, or this week, regarding a topic or a person.

Start with a question or a standard opening. For example: "As a child, I preferred playing with . . ." or: "If I could pick one thing I could do over again, I would . . ." It's a start.

Write a letter to your younger self. Grab a childhood photo and look at the boy or girl: What would you like to tell them? It's a moving exercise. Essential. Or write someone you know a letter you never have to actually mail. Or write a letter to someone you don't know, an idol or a teacher, and tell them how they touched you. Or consider this: If your life was a movie script, how would the plot continue? Write a sequel scene.

Respond to a previous journal entry. Read what you write to yourself out loud and notice how you react to your own thoughts. It's like talking to yourself. A strange experience, but a useful one.

// **Charge Your Happiness Battery**

A tip from my private collection

Now I'm going to share an insight that is personal and such a part of myself that I no longer know exactly when I came up with it or felt it for the first time. But I stockpile happiness to use when I'm sad or when hard or uncomfortable moments present themselves. Like a squirrel hiding nuts and seeds in a hollow tree for when the winter is coming, I store up happiness in my body, for lesser days to come.

I don't see happiness as one large, blissful bubble, but rather as a kind of foam. Moments of happiness exist as tiny bubbles, sticking together to form a larger whole. Each tiny bubble is a moment when you think: *Yes, now I'm feeling it—happiness!* That feeling stored inside the little bubble, that's what I'm trying to preserve.

Have you ever noticed how happiness rises inside your body? I mean the very real physical sensation in your body. I always feel it first right below my midriff, in the form of something glowing that flares up, and in a sudden change in breathing that seems to indicate a kind of "fluffy" lungs. I've begun to call it a "glowing heart." From there, it spreads to the rest of my body. It's an almost tantric sensation, a sparkle that opens up each of the senses: I hear the sounds around me, smell where I am, feel it on my skin, see it with my own eyes, taste its effervescence on my tongue. Such a moment of happiness can appear all at once, out of nowhere. Sometimes you actually can feel it coming, as if all your previous steps have led you to it. You realize that everything as it is, here and now, is exactly right. Here and now, all is perfect and relaxed, calm and beautiful.

Favorite moments: in Costa Rica peddling out on the final day of a surf retreat, bobbing around on the ocean waves amid a spectacular sunset and sea turtles. Falling asleep on the plane, sitting between my two brothers, laying my head first on one shoulder and then the other. Often it's the small moments: hearing a great song on the radio in the car on a cloudless day, the shadow play of a flower on a concrete wall, finding a beautiful sentence in a public library while there's a rainstorm raging outside. In the past, these moments would simply pass. I wasn't really paying conscious attention to them. I just called them "nice" or "pleasant," and life moved on. But these days, when I feel my heart starting to glow, I take notice. *Hey! This is happiness! Let me save this for later!*

How? Well, I take a deep breath through my nose, several times, while holding on to that feeling below my chest for as long as possible, and then allow it to completely subside. In my mind, I direct the feeling all through my body, all the way to my fingertips. I try to anchor this feeling in each of my body's cells; my intention is to store the happiness in my bones. Because I know that it will end. Because, of course, I know that, sooner or later, I will surely get cranky, glum, and angry again. But if I've done a good job stockpiling, on bad days I can return to those moments of happiness by summoning the physical sensation again. It's experiencing happiness in reverse order: first the body, and then the mind. The happiness battery in my bones can recharge me when I've run out of energy. Even in the deepest grief, in the most endless sadness, I have some reserves of happiness to call on.

EVELINE HELMINK

// The Consolation Cardigan

The importance of fluffy things

I have friends—I will refrain from naming and shaming here, but you know who you are—who still sleep with their childhood cuddly toy. Dirty, faded, frayed pieces of stuffed fabric—in many cases, it has become completely unclear whether they represent an animal known to or recognized by scientists. "Scabby" was the name of a friend's stuffed animal; each time I hear that name, I try to nod respectfully (hitherto without success).

Even though I don't have a childhood stuffed animal like that to dry my tears with, I keep to the principle very well. When I see how my son lets out a sigh of relief as he clings to his best buddy, Krokie, after a long day, I ask myself whether there would be a market for adult cuddly toys. If you've ever had a baby and are familiar with the phenomenon of "breast feeding pillows," you might remember how cozy they are.

It just isn't cool for a grown-up to have a bed full of stuffed animals. As a woman, you might get away with it and be deemed "cute" with your childhood cuddly toy. Still, we all grimace in collective horror at that scene from *Love, Actually* when the mousy office wallflower finally takes home the wildly attractive art director and, once he's there, quickly hides her teddy bear under her bed. Watching that scene, I guarantee you that no one will scream: *Don't do it! Just be yourself!* Stuffed animals just aren't sexy, period.

And yet, we know that touch does have a comforting effect for adults as well as kids. I'm not an evolutionary biologist, but it sort of works like this: Our senses allow us to easily move around in the world. Everything we hear, see, and feel (both inside our body and in our surroundings) is sent to the brain, which interprets and translates that information into practical instructions. Touch is an especially important sense; from the first months inside the womb, a fetus is developing sensitivity to physical contact. The receptors in our skin and our fingers literally determine the boundary between our inner and outside worlds.

We don't often pause to take note of the importance of being able to touch something or of being touched. Still, it forms the foundation of our very literal sense of where we belong in the world. The ability to hold something in your hand, to feel it, touch it, is influencing us in all sorts of ways—what we think, how we behave, the kind of opinions we form, and which decisions we want to make. Touch renders the world around us real and tangible.

In psychology, blankets and stuffed animals are referred to as "transitional objects." By means of a sweet illusion created by our brain, an object can offer the same comfort and security as your mother's arms. Cuddly toys are often the first experience of "not me" a child has, so it's no wonder that you can become enormously attached to them. Such a security object meets more or less the following needs of the owner: It represents safety and love; it gives comfort and strength and supports the processing of emotions. For adults, "transitional objects" become less socially acceptable (at least where anyone might see them), but our need for real, tangible comfort doesn't decrease. What does this all boil down to? Well, for one thing, a way to rationalize my attachment to Fluffy Cardigan.

Fluffy Cardigan is soft pink, fuzzy, and also my comfort cardigan. The cardigan and I don't even share that long of a history together. Neither did our paths cross in any special way: I was walking down a busy shopping street, felt cold, happened to spot something pink and fluffy on a rack of sale items in a clothing store. I bought it without trying it on and took Fluffy Cardigan home with me. Fluffy Cardigan is long and oversized, with generous sleeves and deep pockets. You want to make Fluffy Cardigan your home.

Fluffy Cardigan has joined me on faraway travels and has often slept in my bed. I've lost Fluffy Cardigan and found Fluffy Cardigan again. Friends have cursed the damn thing because it leaves thin bright pink fluff marks on dark designer sofas and borrowed coats. I've shed many a tear wearing Fluffy Cardigan. It embraced me when my heart was broken (and never said "I told you so" or "Do you really want to talk about this again?"). And that's why Fluffy Cardigan is a comfort cardigan. And it is a *big* part of my bad days (just like your worn childhood cuddly toy, if you're lucky enough to still have it). Stuffed animal or no, find your own consolation cardigan and wear its protection whenever you need it.

// Because You're Worth It

Opt for quality in everything

Once in a while, but only when I really have to, I will venture into the city center of my hometown, Amsterdam, on a Saturday. It's a place I normally avoid during the weekend because it doesn't present a particularly rosy image of humanity. Stuff, stuff, and even more stuff: bags' worth of it. It just so happens we're living in a time when you can fill your wardrobe, and your kitchen, and your bathroom, and the rest of your home with endless amounts of clutter on the cheap.

I observe the throngs of people hauling their purchases home, and instead of seeing all those packed shopping bags, I see what they symbolize: bandages and painkillers. That's the false promise made by buying and owning: that retail therapy will make you happy and that material things can solve emotional problems. James Wallman says as much in his book *Stuffocation*, adding, "In today's culture, material goods have become substitutes for deep and genuinely meaningful questions. Consumer culture has become a sort of pseudo-religion. It's much easier to focus on questions like 'The blue one or the red one?' or 'Will that go with the top I bought last week?' or 'What will they think if I buy that?' than pondering meaningful questions, like 'Why am I here?'"

Material goods don't make you happy, but at the same time, I also think that having nice things can contribute to your happiness. This may seem to be a paradox, but it isn't. It's simply this: quality over quantity. When I'm having a bad day, I am comforted by the fact that the things I've surrounded myself with don't annoy me or remind me of what I don't want. Things that aren't "right" only take up space, in both the literal and figurative sense. How much more life-giving it is to surround myself with things that genuinely make my life better, more organized, and more beautiful. Better one sharp knife than a drawer full of unused, duller versions of that same knife. Better one soft hoodie to disappear in than fifteen stretched so-so sweaters. Better one really nice shampoo than six half-empty, okay-ish bottles.

Things and products that neither inspire nor serve you tend to drain energy from you. You don't want to surround yourself with subpar stuff, because it will give you a subpar feeling. I want my living space to mirror how I'd like to see my inner world as much as possible and for the two to blend seamlessly. How annoying is it if you, on days that you're already not feeling so great, have to deal with mediocre stuff?

I don't want a lot, I don't want expensive, but I do want quality. It is not so much about money but more about making choices. What do you allow yourself? What do you think you're worth? How do you take care of yourself? Opt for a versatile, razor-sharp kitchen knife. Buy yourself a quality bra in the right size, one that really fits you. Buy a nice makeup brush, generous, comfy towels that dry up well, laundry detergent that smells lovely and is environmentally friendly, a nonslip yoga mat, incense sticks that don't cause smoke, a nice tea mug, a quality pan, a bathrobe to live in. We have so much stuff we don't need. Have your home reflect what you would like the inside of your head to look like. That doesn't immediately make you a hard-core minimalist, but perhaps a bit more of an essentialist.

Is that superficial? Maybe to some people. But not so much, if you ask me. It's about durable, sustainable, and meaningful living. It's about things that will make you happy time and again, objects that serve you and that do what they should be doing. Whenever you have a choice, choosing quality will impart a sense of self-worth and control over your life.

How to Choose Quality

◇◇◇◇◇◇◇◇◇◇◇◇◇◇◇

What are you really buying? Often when I feel the temptation to buy something, I notice that what I really want is to make a desire or experience tangible for myself. A beautiful new notebook? In fact, I'm buying the desire to take time and reflect in beautiful sentences or start over on a blank page. New yoga pants? In fact, I'm buying the desire to move more regularly again. New makeup? In fact, I'm buying the desire to be the kind of woman who has her life in order to the point that she always appears well-groomed. In most cases, I already have enough items to actualize those desires and don't need the purchases at all. Apparently, sometimes all that stands between dreaming and doing is a debit card.

Ground yourself in your preferences. When you do need to buy things, knowing what you love or what gives you a sense of self is the foundation you want to choose from. For example, my favorite colors are the pink of rhubarb compote the way my grandmother used to make it in canning jars, the deep green color of the ocean, and the bright white of an empty page awaiting a pen. Those are colors that soothe me and make me feel at home. When you don't know what you like or what feels intrinsic to you, you are more sensitive to trends and thoughts along the lines of "If I have that, then . . ." To discover what fits you and what is a timeless favorite, you can take a look at the things you would never throw away. What are the colors, textures, materials, and styles that float to the surface?

Clean your house. Get rid of items that no longer have any practical use or meaning to you. Remove the noise: Why would anyone need a pineapple peeler, an egg slicer, an apple corer, and seven different cheese knives?

Make sure things have a permanent place. You'll need to ask whether you still have masking tape, black shirts, or Tylenol less often. On tough days, it saves you a lot of annoyance if you can find your keys, if your chargers are in their drawer like they're supposed to be, and your favorite dress is hanging on a hanger and not crumpled in a drawer somewhere.

Develop a new definition of "value." Is something valuable if it has been collecting dust for three years at the bottom of your closet or if it never catches your eye there on top of your sideboard?

Grant your belongings the right to serve their purpose. Clothes don't want to be in the closet; they want to be worn. Notebooks want to be scribbled in, perfume to be smelled, baking dishes to be cooked in; shoes want to traverse the world. If you can't make that happen for them, give them to someone else.

// Fake It Till You Make It

Sometimes it's good to be a bit ahead of the times

It was a green sweater with an enormous panther head embroidered on the front, studded with sequins and beads. And by green I mean, *bright* green. Kermit the Frog green. Blindingly green. Most definitely an eye-catcher. But one with a hefty price tag. Even on sale, the sweater was priced such that most people would probably go and get a coffee before deciding to buy it. Not my friend Fabienne. She stood in the fitting room wearing the sweater, twirled several times with a look of elation in her eyes. For years, my friends and I have had a tradition of going into town sometime between Christmas and New Year's Eve. Although we've grown older and wiser (something to do with sustainability and discovering that clothing and shoes are less important than we thought), we still always browse the racks, just in case. And there it was, the green sweater. It behooves me to say that it looked amazing on her. But, as we knew, the person admiring it in the mirror was also temporarily out of big work assignments. "Um, do you really need it?" I asked gingerly. What I meant was: "Um, can you afford this right now?"

"Oh," she said, "I'm sure I'll get a gig before long, so I'm buying the clothes I would be wearing if I had a good income. Fake it till you make it!" She cast a final look of satisfaction in the mirror, took off the sweater, and headed over to the register.

Now, I'm by no means making a case for purchases that are over your budget, for impulse decisions, or for bright green sweaters, for that matter (hardly anyone looks good in them) but, oddly enough, sometimes seemingly insignificant events like these can provide you with a major insight. I still remember that moment—the marble shop floor, the panther head on the sweater, and most of all her remark: "Fake it till you make it." Just pretend, and it will become a self-fulfilling prophecy. It sounds easy enough. But I know Fabienne really well, and that's not how she meant it. Fabienne is fierce: At that point she chose what she imagined for herself. The episode with the sweater triggered something in me, and now, a few years later, I can also say what it is: the concept of stepping forward in time. That you lay claim to something that you don't possess yet. Something that hasn't materialized yet.

It's more subtle than the principle of *The Secret*, which wants you to believe that if you just hurl your wish list into the universe with enough force, your wishes and desires will be delivered to your doorstep. It's a certain energy that perhaps generally is more associated with manliness: shouting just that little bit harder than is justified. Perhaps it's a bit American as well: bluffing your way to your goal. The funny thing is that, in doing this, you can sometimes trick yourself in a positive way: Perhaps you *know* that the circumstances aren't right yet—but your brain *will* remember the feelings you gave yourself: pride, satisfaction, self-confidence. The more you dare to do this, the more these positive emotions will become genuine and natural. And the more natural they become, the more they will guide your choices. Laughing is a concrete example of this principle: When you contract the muscles in your face that are essential for a laugh, your brain will receive a signal that it should release endorphins and dopamine.

On bad days, I sometimes think about the bright green sweater. To me it is a symbol: What do I need right now to put something in motion, give it a push in the right direction for later? Am I already living according to what I would want to manifest?

// Radio Mantras

The spiritual benefits of low-brow easy listening

There's no written rule that requires you to speak Sanskrit or mandates that you study a certain number of self-help books or clock a minimum number of meditation minutes to achieve personal growth or a conscious life. Not because it's useless to do those things, but because they're not *required*. It isn't all or nothing; often there's a middle ground as well.

Take mantras, for example. An article in *Happinez* once referred to mantras as "lullabies for the soul," and I can't think of a nicer description. When reciting mantras, you chant words of wisdom that help you to calm your soul, to vibrate off negative thoughts, and to bring positive intentions into the world. You might know *Om mani padme hum*—a well-known mantra in Tibetan Buddhism. There are many different translations, but it is said that the sounds free you of pride, anger, jealousy, and stupidity, and that you can sing it to wish yourself (or someone else) to be freed of suffering and the source of that suffering. But it's not a magic spell.

You can *om mani padme hum* all you like: Without a genuinely felt intention, the words remain hollow. The opposite is also true: Words you genuinely feel and understand can *also* be meaningful. I like to call these radio mantras. In Europe, we have a station called Sky Radio that plays "only the best music nonstop." If you're not regularly listening to it at home, you have surely heard it piped into the back of a cab, a store, or your workspace. Whether they really only play the best music is up for debate, but that's beside the point. In any case, radio stations like Sky excel in easy listening and golden oldies, and at times, that's perfectly fine.

One fine day, I was in a store looking for something, and suddenly a song hit my ear that, for a split second, moved me. If you happen to be holding a hot cup of tea in your hands right now, I'd suggest you put it down, because you might roll over laughing when I tell you the name of the song that so unexpectedly transported me to enlightenment. It was . . . well, um . . . it was "My Heart Will Go On" by Celine Dion.

I don't even know all the lyrics, but that cheesy chorus hit a nerve. Before I knew it, I was going down the rabbit hole. My mind went whizzing through endless tunnels, illogical associations merging into new insights; small eureka moments were exploding like bottle rockets in my soul, and

I landed on an incoherent conclusion that I will spare you—but *also* with a relaxed body and a consoled heart. And, most important of all, in that moment I found this sensation pleasant and fine. I still occasionally hum that song as a comforting mantra. And yes, my repertoire also includes mantras of less questionable reputation.

But remember this: It doesn't always have to be highly intellectual or "officially" spiritual to have meaning. Breathing in a little air will make your practice so much more approachable and lighter. There's no law to determine what is wise and what isn't. Nothing is mandatory; everything is allowed. So go ahead and blast mediocre songs to cheer you up on a bad day. Or binge schmaltzy rom-coms. Or read books that didn't win a single literary prize. I find it wonderful to see how completely random words and images can reach into your soul like the jittery claws of an arcade grabber machine and dig up something to drop into your consciousness like a prize.

// Create Soundtracks for Your Life

Music matters

Music is a language that transcends boundaries—both those separating the people of the world and the one between you and the highest heaven. Music lends everything color, meaning, atmosphere, emotion, and meaning. It is not without reason that people have been using music since the beginning of time as a way to share stories and feelings, to stir up crowds, or to calm them down.

I often think about it in my car, with the rain pouring down and drops converging into mini-rivers flowing across the windshield. Those are the kind of moments when music can be the soundtrack to your life: Will it be a melancholy ballad that makes everything gloomy and hopeless or an up-tempo dance song to the rhythm of the lampposts flashing by? Music colors the story.

You can also fill a space with music as though it were water, your skin the only barrier between outside and inside. You can lose yourself to the music, as they say. It is a way to communicate between your inner and outer world, as well as a form of play. In any case, I am very sensitive to it. On bad days, I impose a strict ban on melancholy ballads. When I need an extra boost, I play ridiculously happy music. And some proper beats during my workout easily make me do ten lunges more than I thought I had in me. I often play classical music in my office, which helps me focus. And when I play the cello or the ukulele, I feel the deep reverberation coming from the sound box next to my heart.

Music is closely related to our body, mind, and soul. Regardless of your age, your culture, or the path you walk, music is healing. It can act as a pain reliever, tranquilizer, or muscle relaxant. Our hearing, like our other senses, is a means to perceive and experience the world around us. You can stimulate and soothe it with sound, and consequently change your mindset. Music affects brain waves that help you reach, and remain in, a certain state of mind.

I sometimes listen to delta waves before going to sleep; they help me fall asleep more easily and deeper. A simple tip for lesser days: Create playlists for each of your possible moods. A playlist to help you reach deeper into your emotions if you feel like letting your tears flow freely. A playlist that is soul-soothing: calm, chill, relaxed. A playlist for when you need energy. A happy playlist. Curate whatever you need. That way you provide your life with your own soundtrack.

You can make your own music too, even without being able to play a single instrument. Sing to yourself. My favorite places? The classics: in the car and in the shower. At the wheel, I furiously scream along to punk songs and belt out ballads while crying my eyes out. I've shamelessly danced to house music and also devotedly chanted mantras. The soul likes to sing, and not every ego enjoys an audience. So that shouldn't be too difficult to arrange.

Singing, like many of the other shortcuts in this book, has long received the scientific stamp of approval. Singing works on the body just like yoga and meditation: It reduces stress and increases the production of good hormones. It bends your breath into unexpected curves, helps express your emotions, and creates vibrations that can invoke a sense of harmony in your body. It's good to let your voice be heard, from the depths of your essence. To make sounds that express something. To growl, to roar, to bellow, or to hum softly. Using your voice for your own well-being is not about auditioning for *The Voice* at all; it's about vibrating an energy you don't need "out of your system" or evoking an energy you actually do need. It is for good reason that yogis love the "ohm" sound, which actually sounds like "a-u-m." It is said to be the primal sound of the universe, in which everything that is comes together. When you sing or chant "ohm," you tune in to that pure energy and allow yourself to resonate with it. So sing, nightingale, sing!

// Art Is Good for You

Museum wellness

When I was about fourteen years old, I was a fan of Picasso. With my wonderfully pretentious adolescent brain, I made a solemn pledge: No matter where in the world I'd end up, if there was a work by Picasso on show, I'd go and see it. On my bedroom wall, works by the great artist hung scattered between Nirvana and NOFX posters, among them a surreal, weeping Dora Maar, Pablo's muse.

I knew something about grief and suffering by fourteen, but I remember that when I stared up at Picasso's work, I *felt* it, without needing to grasp it intellectually. It spoke to me at a deeper level, as only art can. My obsession with Picasso passed, but my love for art remained. Or rather, what remained is the love of what art can do to you.

Museums are safe spaces. Surrounded by art, I feel secure and connected. I feel perfectly calm and content at a Georgia O'Keeffe show at the Tate Gallery in London or looking at the photographs of Patti Smith, taken by Robert Mapplethorpe, in the Kunsthal in Rotterdam. When you're in a museum, time dissolves a little—being in those halls is at least as nourishing as a spa day. Artists provide insight into something all of us are trying to do every day, whether on a personal or universal scale: to experience reality and transform it into something meaningful.

Even the most trivial anxieties can be a source of creation and transformation. Art challenges you to form an opinion about what you find beautiful and what you don't, to be open-minded, to see how creative and expressive your mind is. And art is always truthful. It speaks a universal language that expresses, in countless ways, what pleasure is, what pain is, what love is, what frustration is. Art helps you to reflect on emotions and to express them. A lot of art is the result of artists having to deal with lesser days: Vincent van Gogh, to name an example, wasn't necessarily mister sunshine.

A visit to a museum doesn't have to be pretentious and highbrow. You don't need to be an expert at all. Knowing what the artist meant to say with his work, or being able to place it in its time—that's all great fun, if you're interested, but it doesn't have to be so complicated. My son saw a juicy hamburger sandwich in a work by Marc Rothko. That's fine too—

I believe Rothko wanted viewers to establish their own relationship with his work.

Visit a museum and take your time. Absorb everything you see and examine what it means for you. You don't have to find it beautiful! Resistance and disapproval also sharpen your mind. In his role as John Keating in *Dead Poets Society*, actor Robin Williams says, "Medicine, law, business, engineering, these are noble pursuits and necessary to sustain life. But poetry, beauty, romance, love, these are what we stay alive for."

If all of the aforementioned doesn't interest you, one final encouragement: It's so amazingly quiet in a museum. You can hear yourself think, and sometimes, that's reason enough to go.

There is a light

★ SOMEWHERE ★

LOOK AROUND FOR A MOMENT

// Nature Is a Mirror

Bad days are a part of life

Occasionally, I'm amazed by just how much heartache we cause ourselves over *what is*. Truly everything around us, including our own body, tells it exactly like it is, unvarnished. Step outside, look around you, and you see one big neon sign: *This too shall pass.* In nature everything is impermanent. Everything is evanescent.

When was the last time you were rain-soaked down to your socks? I myself remember it precisely: It was during an editorial staff trip with the magazine on the island of Texel, and we were rushing to catch the ferry back. Above our heads, a rainstorm broke loose, and ahead of me lay endless miles of biking through the dunes. It's strange, what happens in situations like that: At first, you begin to peddle faster—as if you can dodge the raindrops or overtake the clouds. Then, briefly, your mood turns sour as you slowly but surely are getting soaked to the bone. But after that? By the time your pants are sticking to your legs and your hair is draped on your head like thick spaghetti noodles? I had to laugh so hard. I was soaking wet anyway. I was already cold anyway. There was no escape. It's raining. And it will clear up. Ultimately, a simple story.

Once you become aware of all the things going on around you in nature, you have one of the most comprehensive educations you can find, right there, completely free of charge, within reach. And we ourselves are part of it. You *are* that nature. It's just that we often don't act like it. Headstrong little humans, all of us, we think: *It shall not pass. It shall not wither. Love has to be everlasting. Bodies shouldn't turn wrinkly and feeble. The sun should keep shining.* We want the same from the world around us: fresh strawberries in the store year-round, no one is allowed to fall ill, and how come you suddenly get fewer "likes"? There's nothing in nature that blooms 365 days a year—but we are a tough crowd when it comes to that message.

Ignoring the circle of life causes a strange kind of tension in your head and body that can go unnoticed. When you don't pay attention, you run the risk of actually no longer being fully in sync with life. We tend to associate "a new season" with fashion collections, trends in home decoration, and recipes, not with life *itself*. To us, it's complicated enough

EVELINE HELMINK

to go to sleep when the sun sets and to wake up when the sun comes up—let alone to relate the passing of things to ourselves. And that's a shame, because nature is constantly evolving.

Everything has its own rhythm. There's a period of growth, of bloom, of withering, and of stillness. And on a bad day, it's a comforting thought that everything is cyclical, that everything is transient. Maybe the storms of life are raining cats and dogs right now, but hey, it's not going to last forever. Let life happen! We can live spring, summer, fall, and winter—sometimes four seasons in a single day. There are moments during which you are exuberant, and there are times of growing pains and getting closer to your goal step-by-step. There are moments of harvesting what you sowed with your own blood, sweat, and tears, and there are times when everything seems to be in total gridlock (although, in hindsight, that often turns out to be a time of reflection and new insights; mark my words). That balance is necessary. Exert yourself and relax. Grow, bloom. We mirror nature. There's a reason spiritual teachers use nature as a metaphor for personal growth and inner peace so very often.

Sometimes I miss that sense of self-evidence, that moving along with the seasons like you did as a child. As a kindergartener, I made cobwebs from chestnuts (like God's eyes), strung daisy chains, and built snowmen, lips blue from the cold. As an adult, it sometimes seems so much more complicated to stay in touch with nature. But you don't have to cloak yourself in a camouflage outfit and rubber boots to see what She has to tell you. All you have to do is develop a little awareness.

As Mark Nepo observed so astutely, "I keep looking for one more teacher, only to find that fish learn from the water and birds learn from the sky." Look at the trees on your own street: a green haze in spring, neon green in the summer, orange-yellow-brown in the fall, stark black silhouettes in the wintertime. Bring nature into your home: tulips in the spring, chestnuts in the fall. They remind you of the bigger picture. Perhaps a bad day feels like a winter day. But after winter comes spring. Maybe you were completely rain-soaked today. But after rain comes sunshine.

Cliché? Yes. But true. It's the law of nature.

Winter Is Coming

◇◇◇◇◇◇◇◇◇◇◇◇◇◇

Now and then, try comparing your emotional state to the passing seasons. It puts your moods in a larger perspective.

Spring is about germination, about new life, a fresh start, about finding your form, about sowing and growing and awakening.

Summer is about blooming, energy, maturity, connection, feast and abundance, outdoors, and everything taking shape.

Autumn is the time for harvesting, seeing the result, but also for letting go, turning inward again, gathering and saying goodbye and slumbering.

Winter is the time to reflect, to rest, to gain strength, to recharge, to enrich your mind, and to prepare for a new period.

// Flowers as Medicine

An excuse to always have them in your home

I love to always have fresh flowers at home. It's a nice ritual: going to the flower stall, handpicking the most beautiful assortment, bundling it like a casual field flower bouquet in crackling wax paper, then putting it in a vase. Having the satisfaction of being someone who always has fresh flowers in the house, of being someone who finds it worth investing in what wilts. To be someone who—even if only for herself—makes life beautiful. But flowers have an even deeper meaning to me: They are a simple, accessible, and beautifully poetic way of reminding me that everything is impermanent.

In an interview for *Happinez*, Alain de Botton said something that I almost know by heart: "Accept the temporary nature of things. We assume that things we like will remain the same forever. We hope that life is eternal, that our possessions will continue to shine, that our bodies will retain their youthfulness. While we should think about things the way we think about a flower, which has a natural development of budding, blooming, and wilting. Then it is no longer a tragedy. It is precisely in connection with pain that beautiful things get their value."

Whenever you sense a resistance to the ephemeral nature of things, to time rushing forward incessantly and the feeling of having to leave behind people and dreams, walk over to the flower stall. Growing, blooming, and wilting—you can see life passing by. When you really look closely, you'll discover beauty in each phase of existence. The intense color of a wilting petal, the intriguing, whimsical shapes: Flowers on the verge of perishing may actually be at their prettiest. That everything runs its course, and that there's beauty in that, is something to cherish. On top of that, the presence of flowers intensifies your sense of satisfaction, positivity, and connection. Scientific studies indicate that hospital patients who are surrounded by flowers need less pain medication and are more optimistic.

Having living (or formerly living) beings like plants and flowers in your home also connects life inside and life outdoors. It literally brings life into your house—and that benefits your soul, which moves along to that natural cycle. Our houses are often so thoroughly insulated, so soundly built, so static . . . if you didn't feel an inclination to leave your house, the only way the seasons would be measured would be by how high you set your thermostat.

It's no coincidence that flowers have been part of ceremonies and rituals for centuries. Flowers at a funeral are meant as a remembrance of the bloom period. Flowers at a wedding refer to blossoming love. All over the world, you'll find spiritual places with flowers and flower offerings: They represent birth and death, life and the element earth. Flowers are related to feelings, to emotions, and as such, to human existence as a whole.

In Japan, the art of flower arrangement is called *ikebana*. It's a centuries-old tradition rooted in Buddhist flower offerings. Everything revolves around harmony, symbolism, and simplicity. The way flowers are arranged represents beauty and the connection of man with the environment. The tradition follows strict rules and isn't necessarily something to do at home, but the essence is very beautiful: telling a story with flowers that fit your mood of the moment. Don't make it more complicated than it is. Don't see flowers as just another way to glamorize your home, though, but rather as a gift and a sweet lesson for your capricious lesser self. Flowers aren't a luxury; they're a form of sometimes dearly needed self-care.

// **Landmarks Along the Way**

How to measure your state of mind

Before moving to Amsterdam, I took the A1 in the direction of the city on my morning commute every workday, including the section between the Bunschoten/Spakenburg exit and the junction with the A27. Countless times I've been stuck in traffic there. Countless times I saw the sun rise on my way to work and set on my way home. On one side, I saw the slopes of the Utrecht hill ridge on the horizon; on the other, I saw the church towers of Eemnes, and sometimes, on a particularly clear morning, the houses around Gooi Lake. I have seen this landscape in the rain and snow. I have seen its grass shoulders all shriveled up and browned, sighing under a suffocating blanket of heat, but also fresh green, the white mist of a crisp, fresh spring morning lingering over the meadows.

And I often thought: I've seen this so many times, but never exactly like this. What I also noticed was that I was just as changeable as that view.

I've sat in my car completely calm, but also furious. I've sung from the top of my lungs, but I've cried as well. I've seen those same meadows in a mood of great chagrin but also with great optimism. That stretch of road, out of all places, has become important to me. It became a landmark and a memory of how everything keeps passing by, also on bad days. By now, I've been living and working in Amsterdam for years, and I've formed comparable landmarks there, but to me that particular stretch of countryside will always remain connected to the self-examination I was conducting at the time. That practice had nothing to do with a yoga mat or deep meditation; it was just plain old mindfulness as I worked to be present with myself, in my plain old Ford, on the A1, between Bunschoten/Spakenburg and Eemnes. Poetic, not so much.

I called that part of my commute my "car thermometer." It became a natural habit to check the temperature of my soul each time I drove by that view: How am I feeling right now? A moment of mindfulness embedded in my daily routine. And although it's a good idea anyway to regularly take stock of how things are going, this simple habit came with a wonderful side effect: I realized that the routine itself began to offer me consolation. I was stuck there on that miserable stretch of asphalt, but I was *also* carefree or excited. Everything I saw and felt was always in flux.

I knew this for sure because I'd already experienced it. Now I have similarly meaningful places along the route of my bike commute to work: the crosswalk at the Molukkestraat, for instance, where there's a heart-shaped hole carved out of the white asphalt. Can you do a checkup like this each morning during a meditation? You sure can. A landmark, however, is a visual reminder of good times and bad times, and of how those two keep occurring, one after the other, over and over again. In this sense, the streets are literally paved with consolation. Simply relating to the world around me helps me to reflect. When you connect images and places to moments of insights, they become etched in your brain more easily.

Mindfulness Is a Place

◇◇◇◇◇◇◇◇◇◇◇◇◇◇◇

There are beautiful time-lapse videos of sunsets, filmed in one spot on the horizon by installing a camera on a roof and having it take a photo at exactly the same time for 365 days. And there is an artist who has made hundreds of paintings of the sky, always from the same location; Jurianne Matter takes a walk through the heather almost every morning and documents her routine on Instagram. You too can start a project like this, by taking a photo in the same place every day or writing down a note on your phone.

// Go Watch the Waves

About the healthy effects of salt water

Unsure where to go on a bad day? If you ask me, "salt water" should be high on the list. My mom loves the sea; my dad likes lighthouses. For as long as I can remember, they've kept a collection of shells with strange, whimsical shapes at their home, and in his home office, my father has a shelf dedicated to snow globes with small lighthouses inside. Neither my mother nor my father grew up near the coast, but still, even now that my mother is no longer always aware of place and time, the sea instills in her a sense of calmness and happiness. "My mom used to be a mermaid," I like to say sometimes.

I myself didn't grow up by the seaside either, but I was surrounded by heather and lakes. Yet there are only a few places in the world where I truly feel as good and calm—deep, deep to the bone—as on the ocean shore or, in the Netherlands, the seaside. Water that breathes. Water so wide you cannot see the other side. Water that is salty like tears and sweat. It is my quiet place.

I really wanted to learn how to surf, and for *Happinez*, I once wrote a story titled "The Ocean as a Teacher." The ocean is such an accessible place; it's free, always open, and at the same time so intensely soul-soothing. There are no altars and statues, no rituals or scripted prayers, only the wind, the sand, and the horizon. I always feel great awe for the endless, vast body of water that embraces such a large part of the globe, that ripples, and folds, and flows, agitated by the moon, by storms and trade winds, able to propel waves for thousands of miles to coasts far beyond the horizon.

The sound of rolling waves washing ashore, which you can hear on beaches everywhere, is like a lullaby. Sometimes it sounds as if the waves are laughing at me when they break at my feet thunderously; it makes me chuckle. "You are not a drop in the ocean," wrote Rumi. "You are the entire ocean in a drop"—a favorite line of mine because sometimes I can literally feel the ocean inside me: the tides, the waves. We are like tiny oceans.

Salt water reminds us of everything that is timeless and indifferent—and that puts things in perspective. The ocean doesn't judge; it just is. The water lifts you up and embraces you, or it pushes you over,

EVELINE HELMINK

indiscriminately. Floating in salt water, we are all equal. On bad days: Go to the ocean.

Or, if nothing else, look at it on YouTube. Or listen to it via one of those "ocean sounds" soundtracks. Zen master Alan Watts captured the magic of waves and tides best when he wrote: "Although the rhythm of the waves beats a kind of time, it is not clock or calendar time. It has no urgency. It happens to be timeless time. I know that I am listening to a rhythm which has been just the same for millions of years, and it takes me out of a world of relentlessly ticking clocks. Clocks for some reason or other always seem to be marching, and, as with armies, marching is never to anything but doom. But in the motion of waves there is no marching rhythm. It harmonizes with our very breathing. It does not count our days. Its pulse is not in the stingy spirit of measuring, of marking out how much still remains. It is the breathing of eternity, like the god Brahma of Indian mythology inhaling and exhaling, manifesting and dissolving the worlds, forever. As a mere conception this might sound appallingly monotonous, until you come to listen to the breaking and washing of waves."

THE SOUL

KNOWS BEST

<><><><><><><><><><>

A
TAD
ESOTERIC,
BUT
THEY DO
HELP

<><><><><><><><><><>

// Synchronicity: Hints from the Universe

Pay attention to the small things

Your intuition doesn't scream, she whispers. She's subtle, funny, mysterious, and demands attention in the most wonderful ways. The world around you is as it is, so it's our perception that attributes meaning to it. How "awake" you are and the way you perceive is what sharpens your intuition. When you hear a snippet of a song, when your eye is caught by a word, when you instinctively pick something up or are suddenly alert: That's your intuition whispering to you. To understand her language, you need to develop a refined sense of hearing. On hard days, she's a fantastic and indispensable partner.

Of course, you can walk a path of strict nonbelief. Many do so, and it is a life strategy you can grow very old with. The days will be tacked on to days like always; the sun will set and the moon will rise, time after time, nothing to worry about. But it will be a little like snoozing through life. Comfortable, and perhaps it's exactly what you need—but it will never entice you to stray from the well-trodden path, nor will it expand your world. You won't get any meaningful rest, and it won't give you new energy. You'll just keep the status quo. But if you choose to, you can lead an "awake" life, alert and attentive to what's around you. At least that life will be an interesting one.

I can't answer the question "Does coincidence exist?" I'm not completely sure. But I'm allowing myself to accept question marks instead of exclamation points. No scientist, spiritual teacher, or psychologist— no one, including myself—can give a rational and comprehensible explanation for synchronous experience. The good news is that it isn't necessary. Nobody knows exactly how synchronicity works, so we have to put rationality on the back burner. I know only this: Listening to the whisper always takes me to a place where I end up discovering something good: a new insight or inspiration. It has given me courage, consolation, a wake-up call, or a clear stop sign. What would have happened had I not noticed those whisperings? I have no idea. I probably would've continued my life as usual, with nothing to worry about.

But I don't want a slumbering existence. I want to discover, feel, and use my full potential. This is how depth psychologist Carder Stout describes them: "Synchronicities are incidents of spiritual significance that ask us to momentarily dampen our self-obsession and consider the possibility of the divine."

How do you notice synchronicity? For me, it's a strange, weird, and exciting feeling: as if an invisible hand gives me a subtle, little push that throws me off balance, if only for a nanosecond. It's as if time freezes for a moment. With synchronicity, it seems as if coincidence and meaning come together in exactly the same moment and fleetingly spark. As if a direct live connection is being established between one's inner world and something in the outside world. As if the mysterious universe ever so briefly winks.

I myself no longer doubt synchronicity or coincidence. It only takes me a nanosecond to sense whether I need to "do" something with an occurrence or whether it just happens to cross my path. Sometimes something catches my eye and I can't feel anything itching or wrenching. Then I simply see "what is." I intuitively feel if something is meaningful. Sometimes I don't know yet what it is I need to "do" with it. In those cases, I store it in my heart by way of a subtle clue. I have a little junk drawer full of hints there, and occasionally something comes falling out: oh, I see now what I needed that for! Sometimes the energy is strong and clear; sometimes I shrug my shoulders and just wait to find out what the hint was. Sometimes I think that something is significant, and later feel nothing; then I let it go.

Playing Around
with Synchronicity

<><><><><><><><><><><>

Don't think too tritely. Often hints will be subtle, cryptic, to be understood only by you. You might occasionally find a pack of chewing gum in your bag after eating falafel for lunch, but generally it works a tad more subtly than that.

Be careful with rational explanations. Let an observation steep like tea and gradually unfold, but don't force a meaning beyond the one that spontaneously pops up.

Use your senses. The eye and the ear are the usual suspects, but also try to deploy your other three senses. Taste, smell, and touch can also be indicators. Let your senses cooperate as one big synchronicity Velcro tape.

To find hints, you have to more or less know what you want to guide. Shoot a question into the cosmos now and then, and allow yourself to be surprised. Whether you're a manifesting type or not, coincidence follows your attention, and your attention follows your intentions. Occasionally something feels like a coincidence, but it can also be that unconsciously you were already prepared for it.

Trust your intuition when it comes to synchronicity. If something doesn't feel like a coincidence, allow yourself to follow that feeling. If it does feel like a coincidence, do so as well. Trust your unconscious, your first hunches, and your own observation. How other people interpret your experiences is totally irrelevant, as long as you don't cause harm to yourself or others. This is an inside game.

Don't underestimate the power of synchronicity. Although we like to think that all conscious decisions are informed by reason, all the things you experience and observe are equally significant.

// On Dreaming

Messages from your unconscious

I'm a vivid dreamer. A former lover often called me "Josephine" whenever I woke up from a captivating dream—a reference to the biblical Joseph whose dreams predicted the future. This isn't to say that I can predict the future, but boy oh boy, I can sure dream. It's something that began during my childhood, when I already dreamed often and very vividly, and never went away. At times, for me, sleeping is like going to the movies: a dream unfolds, with a scenario, protagonists, and a denouement. In the morning, I sometimes still feel tired, as if I'm leading two lives simultaneously: one awake and one sleeping existence.

People have given me dream encyclopedias, or a friend may scream, "We're so going to google that!" I used to think that most dream interpretation was trite, rational, and slapdash, but I began to think differently about dreams after a conversation I had with dream expert and practical philosopher Hans Korteweg for *Happinez* in 2010. After spending decades studying the subject, he cowrote *Het Droomjuweel* (Dream Treasure) with his daughter. It's a book about how you can use dreams to enrich your life. "Dreams give you insight into who you are at the core," he told me. "The unity of our daily and nightly existence is precisely where the essence of who we are lies."

You can think of "day and night" as an hourglass that you keep turning over. The day flows into the night and vice versa. Likewise, you can start to see your dreams as conversations with yourself. Your dreams show you what's going on, in a free-flowing, creative, and, at times, bizarre form. Call them messages from your unconscious, if you will. Consequently, the interpretation of dreams is more than a matter of "this, therefore that." It is a form of meditation, of mindfulness. Dreams are wonderful self-portraits. When you observe them closely in daylight, you learn more about yourself.

And if you're one of those people who claims that they do not dream, that just isn't true. Countless studies have shown that after ninety minutes of sleep, pretty much everybody reaches a state in which all sorts of things start happening in the unconscious. It's possible you don't remember your dreams; writing down what you know first thing in the morning can help. It might be no more than a shred of a feeling. That already could be the start of a dream log. Even if you remember dreams, however, they won't always be clear.

Often dreams are mysterious, incoherent, unrealistic, fluid, and elusive. Korteweg inspired me to look at a dream as a work of art. Just as Picasso didn't represent the concrete physical form in much of his art, but rather an impression, dreams are an impression too. If a dream touches upon something that upsets you or makes you fearful or sad, it's especially tempting to say, "It's only a dream."

I had a dream once in which I lost someone dear to me, right before my eyes. It feels terrible to wake up with such shock and sadness, and then go through that strange moment when you are no longer asleep but it hasn't quite dawned on you yet that, in reality, the person is still in the land of the living. I've also been tremendously angry at someone in my dream, and that feeling was difficult to shake when we had our first *real* encounter. In such cases, it's easier to say that dreams aren't real. Yes and no. Dreams don't show the daytime reality; most of the familiar faces in your dreams don't represent the *actual* people in your life.

I've learned to look at my dreams in a different, less literal, less clichéd way. I no longer boil down my dreams to platitudes about life, for instance; instead, I connect them to my associations and memories, to places and things in my life. In some dreams, we can see universal symbols for good and evil, love and hate, life and death, but often there's a whole reservoir of things and places that only represent something to *you* because they're connected to a personal experience or memory.

Of course, the question then becomes how often to take something literally. If an old flame makes a sudden appearance, does that mean I still love him? If I dream that I'm drowning, should I start to be extra careful around water? It's tricky to separate subjective and objective reality. Bad dreams on a bad day are even more confusing. Korteweg shared the following rule of thumb: If elements or people in your dream closely resemble reality and match with what's on your *conscious* mind as well, then you should look toward the literal end of the interpretation spectrum. If your dreams feature people or places that have few similarities with your conscious life, then it's more interesting to observe them in a figurative sense.

Dreams don't adapt to the image you have of yourself or how you want others to see you. They don't care about the norms and values of your daytime consciousness, and there are no certainties or blind spots. Therefore, deciphering the messages of your soul requires more than an open and curious attitude; it takes some courage as well. Dreams show you your imperfections, with no consideration for your masks or conditioned attitudes. And yes, that can be annoying and perturbing.

Still, I love the idea of being able to visit my soul cinema at night, knowing that the stories on the screen have something to tell me. It allows me to deal with the narrative presented more freely, in a more associative way. People become archetypes, like in systemic constellations; they represent a feeling or emotion instead of who they are as a person. Situations become metaphors. Dreams provide an interesting route to self-knowledge and a mirror for the soul. So don't let your dreams make you too upset on a bad day; use them as a compass instead.

// About Your Inner Child

Sometimes we need to be our own parents

I'll be honest: When I first heard about the "inner child," it wasn't my cup of tea. To me, the term invoked associations of adults in the fetal position, searching for their mother's bosom under a depressing, dropped office ceiling. Yet, having grown a little older and wiser, I do acknowledge that inner child theories have their merit and can be worth examining, perhaps even more so on bad days. Often the foundation for the way you react and the type of emotions you experience was laid in your early childhood. So if you pay attention to the needs of your inner child, you might discover some interesting triggers for your bad days.

A theme that is closely related to the inner child is "innocence"—the big not-knowing, unfettered curiosity, lightness and security. That's your deepest core, around which more and more rings will form over time, like the trunk of a young tree. When you cut down an old tree, you can clearly see it: a center around which tens of rings have grown. In humans, some rings are created as a form of self-protection. The occasion doesn't even have to be a major traumatic experience; everyday human behavior makes your skin grow thicker too. Some other child plows through your sandcastle, your father doesn't have time for you right now, your mother takes something away from you.

Wondering whether emotions, reactions, or patterns are motivated by your inner child can provide new insights and self-knowledge. Especially when things aren't going your way, you can react "childishly." But instead of compensating for it by putting on a stern mask or hiding in a dark corner, you can acknowledge and explore it. You'll see that the more you give voice to your inner child, the closer you'll remain to your authentic self. That gives you air. And yes, sometimes your inner child needs to be reassured.

I've kept a plaster handprint from when I was a toddler. Now when I put my hand over the cast, the imprint of that little hand almost fits inside my palm. Now and then, when I'm really angry or disappointed, I'll do that. It reminds me of the girl I once was. And the things I can't tell myself, I can say to her: Be quiet, it's okay, don't worry, everything will be all right.

Sometimes people carry with them deeply held convictions and patterns that can stand in the way of a lighter life. For them, it's necessary

184

to first heal the damaged child inside. But the inner child *also* has to do with pure pleasure, being in the moment, the magic of simplicity. Don't forget that, once in a while, it can be a sheer delight to behave like a child, uninhibited by the little voice in your head that disapprovingly whispers "Awkward!" or "Get a hold of yourself." Sometimes I *want* to be childish. I want to play in the surf, to startle someone, not have to worry about all the suffering and all the hassle, but to live in a world that is no bigger than what my senses are indicating. No schedule, no responsibilities. My mood very much improves when I do this.

Our need for play doesn't stop when we reach adulthood. Playing isn't a guilty pleasure; it should have a natural place in your life. Play connects, relaxes, is a source of pleasure, and it awakens you and makes you alert. It's a super effective way to reduce stress and make you forget about all the daily fuss. You can think of many games that can be enjoyed as an adult—games that call on your problem-solving skills and creativity: from foosball to gazillion-piece jigsaw puzzles, from poker to ping-pong. And if you never get to the actual game, make it a habit to live playfully once in a while. Jump the white stripes of a crosswalk. Climb a tree. Go full glitter makeup. Regularly and unapologetically give in to your inner child. It definitely is a shortcut to a lighter life.

// Create Your Own Rituals

Action + meaning = consolation

If the word "ritual" immediately makes you think of incense, ceremonies, or deep devotion, I'm going to encourage you to think bigger. In my eyes, rituals are a simple calculation: action plus meaning. Contrary to a habit or a pattern, ritual acts are performed consciously, mindfully, and with regularity. And what you do gives direction or meaning to your life.

A gratitude journal can be such a ritual. As can lighting a candle before you start meditating, sticking your head out of the window first thing in the morning to take a deep breath, or always giving your sweetheart a kiss before you walk out the door. As you repeat the action, you mark the time. A ritual like that connects you to the here and now, while at the same time, other rituals connect us to what is eternal and everlasting. As if you take a golden thread and mark your timeline with a cross-stitch. The "Love you to the moon and back" my sons and I say to each other before I close their bedroom door at night. On days when they're at their father's, I still always walk by their beds and whisper it. A precious ritual from my childhood is "lucky break day." Every Saturday, we'd go to the grocery store and the market with our father, early in the morning, hoping that it would be "lucky break day." Then our dad would leaf through his agenda and make the joyful announcement: yes. Then we got to pick dessert, for instance, or some snack from the racks near the cash register. It was a ritual between our father and us, and it lent significance to an otherwise trivial routine like getting the weekly groceries. It added rhythm and security, and one of those golden cross-stitches.

Making the mundane valuable—that's what rituals can do for you on lesser days. Your life will become more meaningful because of them. You connect the lesser days to the wonderful ones, which gives you a perspective through time with the addition of routine, rhythm, and form. Rituals are nice when you're calm and peaceful, but they'll become even more valuable when things aren't going so well. When your world is a maelstrom, rituals provide a handhold back to better days.

But what should you *do*? It doesn't have to be epic and riveting. In the large Zen monasteries in Asia, the monks really don't spend as much time meditating as we presume here in the West. Often, in a monastery routine, meditation actually consists of performing everyday tasks. Sweeping, weeding, chopping vegetables for dinner. "Simplicity attracts wisdom," as they say, and every daily routine can turn into a ritual, even watering the plants or taking a shower.

Likewise, some of my healing rituals aren't very exciting. The house where I live now doesn't have a dishwasher, for instance. With sustainability considerations in mind, I was fine not having one; I didn't have any grand, spiritual musings about doing the dishes. But now, it has become one of my favorite mindful rituals: I do the dishes at the very last moment of the day, after I have turned off my phone and dimmed the lights. The repetitious motions, my hands in the warm water, have a calming effect on me, as if my soul is briefly dipped in the warm suds as well. For me, it's the moment to look back on the day and let it go.

In addition to implementing daily routines, you can use ritual to mark or release moments that call for it. Bad days are full of such moments: a rupture, a setback, a change. "Rituals go where words can't come," as one writer put it in *Happinez*. I haven't read a better description anywhere.

Performing a little ceremony or taking a symbolic action can be a perfect way to mark something—say, when you say goodbye or when you want to make room for something new or if there's a shift taking place in another sense, one that requires more than silent observance. A few examples: Try making a fire to throw something into, letting a wish be carried by the wind, releasing something in running water, or burying something deep in the earth. Try drawing an intuition card for yourself, light a candle with a good intention in mind, or sit down in the light of the full moon. When you perform a ritual, you mark an event, grand in its moment, so that the event will be embedded in your soul.

// Muttering a Prayer

Also suitable for atheists

"Please, help me!" Sometimes a hastily muttered Hail Mary, a desperate raising of your hands to heaven or folding them in deep silence and speaking your mind, contains much power. Teacher Elizabeth Lesser wrote this about prayer: "One of the reasons I love prayer is that it is an antidote to guilt and blame. If we are unhappy with the way we have acted or been treated, instead of stewing in self-recrimination on the one hand, or harboring ill will toward someone else on the other, prayer gives us a way out of the circle of guilt and blame. We bring our painful feelings into the open and say, 'I have done wrong,' or 'I have been wronged.' And then we ask for a vaster view—one that contains within it all the forgiveness we need in order to move forward."

Often, the first question prayer raises is what or whom to pray to. I myself was raised in a fairly liberal, culturally Christian ideology, and as a child, I prayed occasionally. I understood that you were allowed to ask for help, but that God wasn't a figure perched on a cloud, let alone a mailman delivering ordered parcels. Nevertheless, I passionately prayed during the weeks leading up to Christmas: "Dear Lord, can I please have a Little Miss Makeup?" Little Miss Makeup was a weird, blond, plastic doll whose shoulders you had to deliberately dislocate to make her ponytail grow longer and on whose face makeup would magically appear when you rubbed it with warm water. I *had* to have her. But because I understood that meanwhile there were wars and famines raging in the world, as well as children who didn't have nearly as much as I did, I figured I had to be reasonable. God had other stuff to do too! So I devoutly followed my prayer up with: "And if you can't, Little Miss Fashion would be fine too." Christmas Eve came, and God didn't answer.

The praying from my childhood was naïve, as are the childhood prayers of most of us. And many people no longer identify with the Christian scheme, myself included. But couldn't you perhaps just sidestep that "to whom" issue? How would it be if the insight that life is bigger, more mysterious, and more elusive than we are able to grasp is enough to experience the power of prayer?

If you do want an entity to address and want to cry out "Hey, to anyone out there willing to listen!" that's fine. If you want something more structured, Bram Moerland, culture philosopher and expert on Gnosticism (Christian mysticism) retranslated the Lord's Prayer from the Aramaic, and I've found the first line a universally excellent address for your soul mail: "O Source of being, whom I meet in what moves me."

Regardless of religious stance, the thing I find most comforting is the universal nature of prayer. We all do it from time to time. The child pose in yoga, for example—the position in which you let your head rest on the floor—is a prayer. You bring your head, your mind, lower than your heart and closer to nature. You lay down your ego for the moment. No matter where in the world, people almost instinctively close their eyes sometimes, their gaze turned inward.

Many spiritual teachers make a distinction between praying and meditating. Praying is being in conversation: articulating your question, expressing your doubts, asking for help and forgiveness. Meditating is listening, being open to the answers, which, in all their subtlety, you often already carry within. In that sense, praying and meditating are the yin and yang of the art of sitting on a pillow.

Author and teacher Geertje Couwenbergh, who has practiced yoga philosophy and Buddhism for years, explained in *Happinez* how a Madonna statuette ended up in her meditation room. She'd noticed that, for certain things, she couldn't rely on Buddha, and that sitting and reflecting didn't suffice. I found her words moving: "The Buddha as mirror, Maria as sponge. For matters that exceed my understanding and ability—the matters of sickness, death, and despair—I need help and mercy just as much as insight, maybe even more so."

Although it may seem like a passive act to send something into the void, you also focus your energy on something you desire. You articulate what's important to you, and where your attention is, your energy will follow. More even than that, though, I find praying on lesser days to be a form of surrender, the acknowledgment of sorrow or absence, or a desire to express something that really stems from your soul. As such, it's also a release of what has been keeping you preoccupied.

Prayer for Beginners

◇◇◇◇◇◇◇◇◇◇◇◇◇◇

What should you say? Whatever you need to say. You may want to complain. You may want to get angry. You may want help. You may want to express your gratitude. You can adapt existing prayers or invent your own. You can use objects too, if that helps ground you: Buddhists sometimes hold a mala with 108 prayer beads in their hands. As you let the chain run through your hands, you establish some sort of rhythm: Each bead represents something you are thankful for or need to get off your chest.

You can also look for ready-made prayers that belong to a tradition that appeals to you online: Native American culture has beautiful prayers, and the internet is full of them. Do your research and hold the right intentions—be wary not to appropriate other cultures!—but if there is something that speaks to you, you can try to find your voice from that place. One day you will find your own words. And then prayer will no longer feel like an empty form, but like a relief or like tapping into an energy. A good prayer makes you feel like you're a little lighter, more connected and heard. If praying doesn't bring you that and instead feels more like a mediocre play or a melodramatic performance, then just don't do it.

// Create a Home Altar

Sacred spaces can be small

It invariably makes my no-nonsense friends chuckle somewhat, but they often spend more than three seconds looking at it: my little home altar. At this moment, it's filled with all sorts of things; it might look random, but to me it's meaningful. A wooden hand manikin from the Tate Gallery, a card from the Inner Compass Cards deck, a golden triangle (amethyst, rose quartz, and rock crystal), a coin with a depiction of a compass rose, and several shells from beaches I've visited, a feather I found in front of my feet, some assorted papers. And a candle that I light if I feel like it. Home altars have slowly become more popular with the rise of meditation, mindfulness, and yoga, and I feel this has everything to do with the need for focus and meaning in our lives that are so busy, busy, busy.

A home altar is a simple way to connect with something outside yourself, whether it be divine, a cosmic energy, or the cycle of life. It might feel a tad esoteric to you, but it can be wonderfully comforting on bad days, and creating one isn't complicated. Whether you want to create a place where you can focus on what you find important or a place for reminiscing and expressing intentions, your altar is yours to build. There are no rules, only suggestions. You can make an altar in the corner of your bedroom, on your desk, in the hallway, or, like me, on top of a sideboard in the living room, a place I picked because I walk by it every day. Fresh flowers, some cherished objects, and perhaps a photograph—and then you're pretty much set.

Here are a few tips and tricks that might come in handy. For one, it's satisfying to mark out a defined space for your altar—for instance, by using a board or a cabinet, or by placing a piece of cloth beneath a certain space. I use a round marble slab. A base like that almost automatically connects whatever you place on top of it. If you want to go to the next level, you can consider what to put where and draw on the elements of nature. Still, I invite you not to overthink these kinds of things.

An altar done right (not that you can truly speak in terms of right and wrong here) is ever evolving and therefore *never* has to be perfect. Your altar itself shouldn't become sacred. It is a means. A tool. You add something, you remove something, refresh the flowers, place a note on top for a change. You can celebrate the changing seasons on your altar, or decorate it with inspiring images you've ripped out of magazines, et cetera. Precisely by being so devoted to it, you charge your altar with your own energy and attention. The most beautiful altars are those that mirror the personality of their creator.

// Living in the Present

It's not the same as #yolo

"Living in the now" is an often-heard adage in spiritual circles. As I wrote at the beginning of this book, it might be the key lesson in pretty much every kind and flavor of spiritual practice: flowing along with life *as it is*. And this *as it is* can only be found in the present moment. The most famous figurehead of the power of now is unquestionably Eckhart Tolle, who has written worldwide bestsellers on the subject. Time is an illusion, he argues, and the only way to find relief is to be fully present in the moment. Freed of stories from the past and projections onto the future, life will become more effortless. Pain, desire, doubt—they stem from worries about what has happened and what could happen. In the now, however, your attention presents you with what you do, feel, and think. On lesser days, you have three options, roughly speaking: stepping out of the situation, changing the situation, or accepting the situation.

Being in the moment, the now, can really put your trouble in perspective, give you comfort and air. "Let's cross that bridge when we get there," I like to reassure myself or others whenever there's a restlessness about all the things that possibly could go wrong in the future. Often enough, life runs a totally different course than I expect, and I have long learned that it usually is a waste of energy to get all caught up in "what if" scenarios. At other moments, I'll put things in perspective: "Water under the bridge!" It's already over, passed, and intangible. You shouldn't spend your energy on the things you could've done differently; you can't time-travel and relive the past.

But what if you really don't want to be in the present moment? On a lesser day, you might actually want to book a one-way ticket to a place far away from this fabled "now." Because the present moment is painful, because you had better plans for this day, because the now is ruining your mood. Sometimes you simply are unable to keep your attention focused on the present. Then the present suddenly no longer feels like an open space but rather like a cage you have to force yourself to enter with all sorts of mental gymnastics. It isn't surprising that living in the now is hard, nor is it something you should feel bad about. Our brain uses looking back and looking forward as survival mechanisms. They put your body and mind in a state of alertness.

"Past performance is no guarantee of future results." Really? Our brains happen to think otherwise. We are hardwired to store everything we experience, consciously and unconsciously, for future reference. Based on our experiences, our brain devises smart strategies, which in itself isn't a bad thing, as devising strategies can also form the fuel for innovation and creativity.

If you can't manage to be in the present in a calm and natural way, it might help to see the now as the pendulum of a clock, swinging back and forth between past, present, and future. Eventually the pendulum will return to the center. Seen like this, living in the present moment is only natural. It's the place where everything originates and to which you can always return. Your home base. Each time you feel tangled up in the past or lost in the future, you'll return to the center. Without judgment or obligations.

Living in the present moment definitely *isn't* about a shallow #yolo (you only live once) attitude. Living like there's no tomorrow can quickly escalate into self-destructive behavior, ranging from eating half of that second pint of Ben & Jerry's (what difference does it make?) to other, way more ill-advised decisions. When you live from one thrill to the next to feel you're alive, you will likely achieve the exact opposite. Thrill seeking is a diversion, a way to be anything *but* present, a way to avoid having to show up in your own life. When you willfully live outside of time, you drown out or numb feelings that are demanding your attention. Living *in* the moment is something different from living *for* the moment.

// The Moon Did It

Sometimes you have to look a little higher

On my right foot, I have a tiny tattoo of the moon. I got it in a tattoo shop near the ocean, which breathes to the rhythm of the moon's gravitational pull, during a time of back-to-back bad days. People often talk about the moon cycles as a reflection of our own life cycles: We watch as it is born as a new moon, waxes to its brightest, then wanes. There's something about that rhythmic constancy that appeals to me. It's why I wanted to wear the moon image on my skin: to remind me of the promise of change and ongoing cyclical motion.

For the realists among us, saying that you feel a connection with the moon is divining rod and tinfoil hat territory, which is rather strange, if you think about it. Those who like to explain everything can hardly deny the effect the moon's pull has on the earth. Nearly two-thirds of the human body is water. So it's not such a strange thought that the moon, which pulls and pushes the oceans and causes tides to ebb and flow, also affects us. We aren't separate from creation; we are part of it. We are an integral part of the system as a whole.

Especially when things aren't going your way, a ticking clock feels like an enemy. Another hour goes by without you peeling yourself off the couch; another ten minutes and you still haven't taken that shower. Moon time is less harsh to us—it's more poetic and forgiving.

It's a cyclical time that always returns to the start, again and again and again. When you live with the moon, it's never "game over" and always "try again." The moon dictates the rhythm of day and night, which has been the same for an eternity, but she herself changes constantly: waxing and waning. This pattern—new moon, first quarter, full moon—emanates consolation.

Women, in particular, are sensitive to the moon's energy. We all have a dedicated antenna built in: the average menstrual cycle and the time it takes the moon to orbit the earth are about the same: twenty-eight days. "Menstruation" has a Latin root, the word *mensis* ("month"), which is in turn related to the Greek word *mēnē* ("moon"). You might be a little more emotional as you approach your menstrual flow (the technical term is "menses"); perhaps your body retains more liquid. Maybe you have trouble falling asleep and your nights are more restless. All of this, of course, is not helpful on bad days.

But there is a constant and wonderful aspect of the moon: Regardless of where you are and who you miss, at night each of us is looking at the same moon. It never leaves you behind, no matter who or where you are.

Moon Inspiration

◇◇◇◇◇◇◇◇◇◇◇◇◇

NEW MOON
time to let go and start over

FIRST QUARTER
time for courage, change, and manifestation

FULL MOON
time of abundance and harvesting what you have sown

THIRD QUARTER
time for clarity, choices, forgiveness

// Constellations for Dummies

Make it insightful

On tough days, I can feel lonely, even when I'm surrounded by people. It's a loneliness that's hard to explain. It's not so much about the physical absence of others but rather a sense that there's no one who sees me in full, down to the depths of my soul. As if I'm an island among islands or a snowflake that doesn't stick to anything. I can free myself of this feeling by remembering that each of us is part of a larger whole, a complicated cosmic fabric in which everything and everyone has their own place. We're endlessly and eternally connected: Nothing is new; all of us are made up of reused molecules and atoms, and nothing is separate. Being part of a larger whole, however unremarkable it may make us, provides context. It offers the chance to choose a slightly bigger perspective now and again, despite what happens to you or which lesson life is casting in your direction.

The objective of systemic thinking is recognizing context. Who you are and how you typically respond to adversity or chaos have been shaped in part by the system in which you live. It provides clarity to look at what is keeping you up at night in light of a bigger picture. Zooming out adds space.

One of the fundamental systems is that into which you are born, your family. The presence or absence of your parents, grandparents, siblings shapes who you are from an early age. These are the people who teach you what is "normal" and what isn't, what is desirable behavior and what isn't. Like little baby bats, we're sending signals to our surroundings. Those signals bounce off the people around you and shape your world. Your family is the first place where you receive (or don't receive) love and gain experience with security, self-confidence, loyalty, and harmony.

And whether or not you believe you can connect with your ancestors, their lives too will trickle down from generation to generation and shape who you are (there are immensely complicated books you can read on the subject, but you can also watch Pixar's *Coco* to get an idea). Maybe you can come up with a motto for your family philosophy: "In our home, we don't let anybody tell us what to do" or "In our family, we just don't talk about it."

These are the types of convictions that, consciously or unconsciously, you will carry with you in your own life and inform the choices you make as

198

an adult. As you look at negative emotions on bad days, it's worthwhile to examine which of the feelings or convictions that underlie these days are in fact *yours*, and which more or less accidentally have stuck with you along the way. Stories like these can also be handed down from other contexts, such as your school, your group of friends, your colleagues, or any social groups you belong to. Each group of people develops some sort of shared identity—"We like to go out and party," "Weird clothes are not done," or "Keep your complaints to yourself," to name but a few obvious codes—but which of those really feel intrinsic to you? How do you relate to the systems you're a part of? Which of the things you've picked up actually don't serve you at all? Is there anything you'd rather shed in order to live a more authentic and pure life?

You can examine this with constellation work, which offers a concrete method to illuminate how you relate to and feel about others, to help you determine whether those relationships and feelings actually feel right, and to try out how it would feel if you'd shift things around. Normally, you'd do this under the guidance of a professional. It's pretty intense to lay yourself bare like this in front of a group of people, often strangers, who then visualize your system.

It doesn't immediately *have* to be the real deal, with actual people and spectators, however: I myself have sparked quite a few new insights by setting up constellations using Lego figures (yes, really!), and that felt intimate and safe. Oddly enough, those figures, with their yellow heads and square hands, provided clear insights that identified burdens from my family soul that I was carrying around and showed how they informed my behavior and thinking.

You too can make constellations for dummies at home, by yourself, without pulling out all the stops. When you physically map out a personal constellation, you can simplify for home use the somewhat complex principle that we all are part of an interdependent system. Through visualization, you might get a better understanding of what isn't flowing, which can give you a little breathing room on a lesser day. You can do this anytime, using all kinds of props. Perhaps you'll find this exercise useful.

Make Your Own Kitchen Sink Constellation

Step 1: Formulate a question. As always, the more concrete, the better. "Why am I afraid to . . ." or "Why do I feel insecure when . . ." or "Why am I so pissed off . . ." et cetera.

Step 2: Write down your question, draw a circle around it, and draw spider legs on it with stripes. At the end of each line, write a description of something or name someone who somehow plays a role for you in this issue.

Step 3: Find representatives. These can be Lego figures, but also pieces of paper with names on them or drawings, stones, flowers, socks, if necessary—it does not really matter as long as you can assign meaning to it.

Step 4: Arrange the objects around the problem in a way that feels right. Then quickly consider a series of questions: Who or what is close to your skin? Who or what is behind you? Who or what is watching from afar? Who or what is blocking something? Try not to think about each one for too long; do it quickly and intuitively.

Step 5: And then? Well, a little philosophizing. You have just materialized your issue, and that can make things visible and change the way you perceive it. Is what you see right? Have any eye-openers come to light? What should be moved? Play with it.

Step 6: When you move things, how does it feel? Does the new configuration or constellation give new perspective? Does it feel lighter?

Think of this process as a way to direct your thoughts. And if it doesn't work for you? Then you have at least diverted yourself by playing a little game.

// Wabi-Sabi

Celebrate the cracks and fissures

With the number of serums, lotions, and creams for preventing or removing spots and pits that we all stock on our bathroom shelves, you would almost think that a smooth and wrinkle-free body is the holy grail of living a long and happy life. Our love for beauty runs deep and can, to a certain extent, be explained: Our human brain has become hardwired to see perfection as nonthreatening. What's easy on the eye is also reassuring to a mind that is still inherently preoccupied with survival. We may have taken it a bit too far, though: The fruit we eat is flawless and shiny, the stuff we surround ourselves with is flawless and shiny, and we expect to appear in our bikinis equally flawless and shiny. Bluntly put, perfection is the option we most prefer, and imperfection is for losers.

What this thinking *actually* does, though, is throw you off balance. It disrupts your harmony with time, with nature, and with your own soul. That is why we have trouble coping with bad days: They catch us by surprise. Why has life suddenly become unpleasant, imperfect, or ugly? How do I make it perfect?

The Japanese ideal of *wabi-sabi* offers an alternative to this perfectionist mindset, and it really is an eye-opener. It can be easy to forget how much beauty there is in simplicity. The word *wabi* is hard to translate, but it refers to simplicity, stillness, and elegance—for example, simple shapes, in which the maker's hand can still be recognized. *Sabi* is the beauty that comes with age: patina, cracks, rust, or moss, elements that tell the story of time and honor the life of an object.

Wabi-sabi represents the essence of life, the cycle of nature; it represents space and time. In essence, applying *wabi-sabi* to your own life comes down to embracing the impermanence of things—not always wanting everything to be perfect, for example, or surrounding yourself with things that genuinely are a part of the course of your life and that remind you that everything is of a temporary nature.

Aren't people with a little frayed edge often much more interesting than smoothed-out types? And aren't the scratches and cracks on your things what make them really yours? Celebrating imperfection in a self-evident way makes it less difficult to shrug off those scratches and cracks, because they are just part of life. It isn't the end of the world. The rings on your tabletop are also a memory of a table full of friends, and the stretch marks on your breasts record your growth from girl to woman. Such rings and marks may not represent beauty in the classic sense, but they're beautiful in another, unique way: They possess the beauty of imperfection.

In the *wabi-sabi* aesthetic, many things are deliberately *just* a little off balance. Take the teacups in the traditional tea ceremony: They are intentionally irregular to remind us that nothing in life is perfect and permanent.

There are three simple truths in *wabi-sabi* philosophy:

Nothing is permanent.

Nothing is ever finished.

Nothing is perfect.

Your imperfections make you who you are. Think about your handwriting, with all its crazy curls or slanted lines. It is precisely in that imperfection that you express what makes you *you*. The first fine wrinkles near your eyes, your smile lines. The first fine silver hairs, the scar on your skin. A soul that carries a life full of stories—that's perfect imperfection.

Looking at the world around you and at yourself like this will make your lesser days milder. You cannot copy, force, demand, or buy it—it's an attitude of surrender and acceptance. You just have to wait and let it happen. In an inclusive life, one in which everything is allowed to unfold, everything belongs: darkness and light, intact and cracked. And there— there is where your freedom lies.

what
feels
like
THE END

is often
THE BEGINNING

★

// A Final Thought

Before we part ways, could you please make me a promise? Promise me that this book won't languish on your nightstand—because this is a book that needs to be lived with, and lived in. It wants stains between the lines, chocolate smudges and splotches of wine or tears (from laughing or crying; I'll leave that to you). It wants you to dog-ear the pages you may wish to read again. It wants scribbly little handwritten notes in the margins. Maybe you can add your own tips and reminders about what you've discovered helps you most on the bad days.

   Because about those bad days . . . they're here to stay. I hope that by now this isn't a disappointment to you. I wholeheartedly hope that you've lost the urge to hide, fix, or numb those bad days, and I hope this book has assured you that all emotions, the good and the bad, are essential guides for you and your happiness—although some of them do a poor job presenting themselves as useful or beneficial. I hope you've learned that you are so much stronger and also softer than you've allowed yourself to be so far.

   You are truly courageous for allowing yourself to explore the bad days.

   Sometimes we need to break in order to really heal. Sometimes we have to fall to gain a new perspective. Sometimes we cry just to water the dry earth to help new seeds of happiness germinate.

   I'm really proud that you honestly answered no the other day when that person asked if you were okay. And that you smiled, knowing that you've got this. Because you do.

   With love,

   Eveline

// Acknowledgments

Writing this book was a lonely process, involving many Sundays spent wearing leggings and sweaters and not seeing a single soul, endless evenings sitting in the Amsterdam Public Library, surrounded by cramming students. Stolen moments on busy Wednesday afternoons. My escape to Los Angeles in February 2018, where I traveled to find inspiration and hours of undisturbed writing, was unexpectedly colored by my mother's admission to a nursing home. It was a very painful period for me and my family. And it wasn't the only time writing *The Handbook for Bad Days* was accompanied by actual lesser days. You can safely call it participatory authorship.

But I was never alone. I would like to thank my two sons. I found "You will finish your book for sure," scribbled on a Donald Duck tear-off calendar page, on my pillow one night, with a heart-eyed smiley added. Pepijn, you sweetheart, I love you and your observing eyes so much. And then Seger, who every other day exclaims: "This is the best day of my life!" I equally love you, and your ability to discover lightness in everything. Thank you, Mom and Dad, for your continuous support and for providing an unconditional home. Even when I was making choices you didn't necessarily understand, there was always love. I've come to appreciate that, contrary to being cheesy, it's in fact a great privilege to hear again and again how you love me and are proud of me. And thank you to my big brothers, Jeroen and Matthijs, who are always there for me—and probably know me better than anyone. With you on either side of me, I always feel safe and carried.

Thank you, Allard. I am thankful that we handle our friendship so cautiously. Our sons couldn't have wished for a finer father.

Thank you, friends whom I can call in the middle of the night. I love all of you dearly, but I'd like to give a special shout-out to Fabienne, Kim, and Tess, who on the worst of bad days came by to paint my ceilings while singing, were willing to hear the same story ad infinitum, and next to whom I could also just sit in silence for hours on end, if necessary.

Thank you colleagues and freelancers at *Happinez*, with whom I've spent years of exploring the most essential, wonderful, and meaningful sides of life in all its aspects. This workplace has brought me so much. And thank you, Adrienne and Marije, aka "the mothers."

Thank you, Lisette, for a last-minute and frank mail exchange. Thank you for all the wise, inspiring, quirky, brave women and men I've met on this path. Yes, you.

Thank you, Martine, at Kosmos Publishers. I wouldn't have wanted to do it with anyone but you. Thank you, Joris van Wijk, for filling my heart and soul with a twist of rationalism. Thank you, Jan, for your patience and alertness. Thank you, Maaike, for your efforts to promote this book. And a standing ovation for Annelinde, the best art director I know, who always manages to exceed my imagination!

Thank you, Victor Verbeek and Marleen Reimer, for your thoughtful, insightful translation.

Thank you, Julia Foldenyi, at Shared Stories. I'm grateful for your support and guidance, and without you, this edition would never have been possible.

Finally, thank you to the whole team at Tiller Press for your outstanding work to bring this book to new readers. I'm so grateful to each of you, most especially Hannah Robinson, to whom I owe special thanks as my editor. Thank you for the love and care you gave my manuscript—improving and clarifying it, even in translation. What a great privilege to be edited and published by someone with so much passion for all aspects of my work!

// **Sources and References**

I included quotations from the following authors, teachers, and/or books:

Maya Angelou, *I Know Why the Caged Bird Sings* (New York: Random House, 2002).

William Bloom, *The Power of Modern Spirituality: How to Live a Life of Compassion and Personal Fulfilment* (New York: Little, Brown, 2011).

Julia Cameron, *The Artist's Way: A Spiritual Path to Higher Creativity* (New York: J. P. Tarcher/Putnam, 2002).

Pema Chödrön, *When Things Fall Apart: Heart Advice for Difficult Times* (Boston: Shambhala, 2020).

Geertje Couwenbergh, *Zin*, 7th edition (Utrecht, NL: AnkhHermes, 2019).

Davidji, *Destressifying: The Real-World Guide to Personal Empowerment, Lasting Fulfillment, and Peace of Mind* (Carlsbad, CA: Hay House, Inc., 2015).

Clarissa Pinkola Estés, PhD, *Women Who Run with the Wolves: Myths and Stories of the Wild Woman Archetype* (New York: Ballantine Books, 2003).

Elizabeth Gilbert, *Big Magic* (New York: Riverhead Books, 2015).

Bernard Glassman, *Bearing Witness: A Zen Master's Lessons in Making Peace* (New York: Bell Tower, 1998).

Natalie Goldberg, *Writing Down the Bones: Freeing the Writer Within* (Boulder, CO: Shambhala, 2016).

Aldous Huxley, *Brave New World* (New York: Harper Perennial, 2006).

Rutger Kopland, *Collected Poems* (Amsterdam: Van Oorschot, 2015).

Hans Korteweg, *Het Droomjuweel: de rijkdom van dromen in ons bestaan* (Utrecht, NL: Kosmos, 2008).

Elisabeth Kübler-Ross and David Kessler, *On Grief and Grieving: Finding the Meaning of Grief through the Five Stages of Loss* (New York: Simon & Schuster, 2005).

Mark Manson, *The Subtle Art of Not Giving a F**k: A Counterintuitive Approach to Living a Good Life* (New York: HarperOne, 2016).

Helen McDonald, *H Is for Hawk* (New York: Grove Press, 2015).

Mark Nepo, *The Endless Practice: Becoming Who You Were Born to Be* (New York: Atria Books, 2014).

Inez van Oord, *Als je leven een cirkel is, waar sta jij dan?* (Utrecht, NL: Kosmos, 2015).

Gretchen Rubin, *Better than Before: Mastering the Habits of Our Everyday Lives* (New York: Crown, 2015).

Sharon Salzberg, *Lovingkindness: The Revolutionary Art of Happiness* (Boston: Shambhala, 2004).

Sharon Salzberg and Robert A. F. Thurman, *Love Your Enemies: How to Break the Anger Habit & Be a Whole Lot Happier* (Carlsbad, CA: Hay House, Inc., 2013).

Cheryl Strayed, *Tiny Beautiful Things: Advice on Love and Life from Dear Sugar* (New York: Vintage Books, 2012).

Max Strom, *A Life Worth Breathing: A Yoga Master's Handbook of Strength, Grace, and Healing* (New York: Skyhorse, 2010).

Shunryū Suzuki, *Zen Mind, Beginner's Mind: Informal Talks on Zen Meditation and Practice* (Boston: Shambhala, 2006).

Eckhart Tolle, *The Power of Now: A Guide to Spiritual Enlightenment* (Vancouver: Namaste Publishing, 2004).

Lynne Twist, *The Soul of Money* (London: W. W. Norton, 2017).

James Wallman, *Stuffocation: Living More with Less* (New York: Viking, 2015).

Alan Watts, *Out of Your Mind: Tricksters, Interdependence, and the Cosmic Game of Hide-and-Seek* (London: Souvenir Press, 2019).

I used a quote from an interview with Jack Kornfield that appeared on the website www.lionsroar.com. Jack is the author of books such as *After the Ecstasy, the Laundry: How the Heart Grows Wise on the Spiritual Path* (New York: Bantam Books, 2001).

I quote Harvey Mindess, whose writings include *Laughter and Liberation* (Abingdon-on-Thames, UK: Routledge, 2011).

I quote words attributed to Rainer Maria Rilke. A good place to start with Rilke is *New Poems: An Anthology*, 2nd edition (Amsterdam: Rainbow Essentials, 2016).

I quote from Cheryl Strayed, *Wild* (Amsterdam: Rainbow Essentials, 2018).

Not quoted in this book but worth checking out (and there's so much more):

Brené Brown, *Rising Strong: How the Ability to Reset Transforms the Way We Live, Love, Parent, and Lead* (New York: Random House, 2017).

Glennon Doyle, *Untamed* (New York: Dial Press, 2020).

Elizabeth Lesser, *Broken Open: How Difficult Times Can Help Us Grow* (New York: Villard, 2005).

John C. Parkin, *F**k It: The Ultimate Spiritual Way* (Carlsbad, CA: Hay House, Inc., 2014).

Sophie Sabbage, *The Cancer Whisperer: Finding Courage, Direction, and the Unlikely Gifts of Cancer* (New York: Plume, 2017).

Websites
www.elephantjournal.com
www.lionsroar.com
www.risingwoman.com
www.goop.com
www.dictionaryofobscuresorrows.com
www.ted.com

And of course, I shouldn't forget the fifteen volumes of *Happinez*, from which I keep a collection of thoughts, words, sentences, and insights in my heart. Published by WPG Media, Amsterdam; www.happinez.nl.

// Illustration Credits

Gun: Shutterstock image 1022250880
Dragonfly: Shutterstock image 1011228235
Scorpion: Shutterstock image 49395010
Skull: Shutterstock image 468765833
Key: Shutterstock image 1280614108
Octopus: Shutterstock image 490099039
Lighthouse: Shutterstock image 772902913
Eye and Tears: Shutterstock image 770350678
Tiger: Shutterstock image 650630500
Sword: Shutterstock image 521904523
Rose: Shutterstock image 489709675

// About the Author

Eveline Helmink is a journalist and writer living in Amsterdam. She is an editor in chief at the international media brand Happinez, which shares insights and inspiration for personal growth and a meaningful life. Follow her on Instagram @Eveline.Helmink.